Healing Pain, Anxiety, and Inflammation Without Drugs

The Science Behind Natural Medicine

Evelina V. Sodt, PhD
December 2019
ISBN: 9781671933149

Organic Living Publishing

Acknowledgements

To my kind husband, who supports all of my crazy ideas, and to my precious daughter, who is the reason for it all.

Table of Contents

Introduction to the autonomic nervous system...5

Background...10

Socio-economic factors and emphasis on the sympathetic nervous system...17

Stress and its effect on our bodies...20

The importance of parasympathetic care...25

The biophysics of pain...37

Acupuncture...40

Needle-free acupuncture...45

Phototherapy science and research...48

The vagus nerve...58

Ultrasound gua sha...60

High frequency...63

Nutrition and its effects on biological processes...69

The mind-gut connection...76

Quantum medicine...88

The anti-inflammatory diet (food regimen)...107

Managing expectations...114

My 3-day juice detox...116

The role of PT…119

Treating the body as a whole…122

References…126

Introduction to the autonomic nervous system

One seldom stops to think about the biological processes within our bodies as we go about our daily routines wrapped in noise, rushing around, scurrying to find presentations, going over points for the next meeting or handling a needy boss. This mundane quiet desperation is often disguised as duty. And there are days of the happy variety of course -- getting ready for graduations, weddings or just looking forward to spending time with someone we haven't seen in a while.

Prompted by a TED lecture, on occasion, we might watch an insightful presentation on the illusory nature of life and the power of the mind as the ground for reality. Naturally, the mind cannot process this type of abstract thinking no matter how many quantum equations point to the math as the ultimate arbiter on the quest for empirical evidence. But perhaps, we process it subconsciously. Science and philosophy have long regarded mental life as conscious in nature, going back to Descartes' *cogito eres sum*, but now the scientific community struggles to define even the term "conscious." Today it is being separated into sub-processes defined as controllable, intentional, serial/consumptive and accessible to awareness.

The ubiquitous yin-yang polarity (thesis and antithesis) is seen everywhere in nature, even in the balance of our autonomic nervous systems. On one hand, we have the sympathetic nervous system response -- a fight-or-flight reaction that enables us to confront or run away from a dangerous situation -- on the other, we have the often overlooked, but absolutely vital parasympathetic system, the opposing force that dismantles the stress. To make the matter even more complicated, we humans, have come up with this idea of on-the-go social structuring, school rules and workforce participation, which encumbers every autonomous biological process with a barrage of continual activities and little or no downtime. The recharge mechanism bestowed upon the human bot, through its amazing parasympathetic system, has been abandoned, forgotten, ignored and malnourished. And that is why it is there -- to help us cope, take a break, heal, re-energize, digest our food, relax, breathe in life and smell the roses. Instead of recognizing the parasympathetic system as our gifted healer, society teaches us not to take its gifts, making its use synonymous with laziness, lack of ambition, poor upbringing, even irresponsibility.

So what is the autonomic nervous system that holds those two responses -- the sympathetic and parasympathetic? Is it simply a set of neurons that mediate internal homeostasis without conscious intervention or control? A theologian may postulate that it is merely the physical representation for the ground of one consciousness, flowing down from the Divine. A physicist may define it as a quantum reality with dualistic nature -- one at work and one at rest. There is a poetic rhythm in the universe, a Big Bounce (Big Bang -- expansion; and Big Crunch -- contraction) an ebb and a flow, an omnipresent expansion and contraction, matter and antimatter, inhalation and exhalation...a heartbeat!

Once an objective view of the autonomic nervous system is procured, judgement can be suspended for a bit. The parasympathetic system can be given an equal place on the podium of autonomic responses and its importance can be celebrated. And when it comes to rejuvenation, restorative processes and self-repair, the parasympathetic system is ruling class.

As our internal organs control homeostasis (the return to balance) the parasympathetic nerves maintain a number of progenitors for organogenesis. What that means is that impaired adult organs regenerate with the help of parasympathetic cells. Injured organs actually do not self-repair after parasympathectomy (the removal of all or part of the parasympathetic nervous system). That is particularly visible after damage from irradiation. A study done at the Cell & Tissue Biology Department at the School of Dentistry, UCSF in San Francisco, for example, showed the vital role of parasympathetic response in epithelial tissue self-repair. Mouse salivary glands were targeted for parasympathectomy because adult human salivary glands also have reduced parasympathetic innervation when damaged by irradiation. It is common knowledge that the parasympathetic system is critical for the proper functioning of the digestive system, the urogenital organs, the pancreas, the cornea, the prostate, lacrimal and salivary glands, and much, much more. This study, however, focused on parasympathetic response and its influence on tissue regrowth proving beyond doubt that the parasympathetic system also modulates morphogenesis.

The study discusses other factors and proteins as novel methods to increase parasympathetic response, while this book focuses on natural parasympathetic enhancement technologies used to minimize mental and emotional stress to enable the body to achieve parasympathetic response. Keeping the sympathetic system engaged at all times strongly compromises the body's ability to regenerate, recover, and maintain health.

Background

The topic of parasympathetic impairment is not only ubiquitous, it is also close to my heart. I didn't sleep from 2007 to 2011. At least it seemed that way. Damaged by the stresses of the corporate world, I sought solace from a racing mind drowning in chronic exhaustion, brain fog and maddening insomnia. Anti-anxiety medications were not an option for me. There was no willingness on my part to welcome a potential lifelong addiction. Out of pure desperation, I turned back to my roots. The answer? Medicinal herbs. I started taking an *Artemisia vulgaris* (mugwort) tincture. The effects were wonderful and immediate. I was encouraged...and then quickly discouraged, as my body built tolerance only in a few short weeks. I also took *Hypericum perforatum* (St. John's wort), *Valeriana officinalis* (valerian root) and *Nepeta cataria* (catmint) with similar results. The hours of internet research led me to nutrition and the mind-gut connection. Dr. T. Colin Campbell's book The China Study: The Most Comprehensive Study of Nutrition Ever Conducted and the Startling Implications for Diet, Weight Loss, and Long-Term Health seemed to have answers. I took the certification classes through a Cornell University program and I changed my diet. Within a month, amazingly (I still had a healthy dose of scepticism), my entire life was changed. I started sleeping ... deeply, soundly, restfully. The biggest surprise came about when I realized that the chronic low-level achiness in my joints had gone away, the inch-wide layer of psoriasis in my hairline had vanished. Whole food plant-based nutrition became salvation for me and I felt like I wanted to help everyone who could relate. There are no words I can use to express my support for greatly reducing animal products and processed foods from one's diet as a healthful choice. That said, I don't discount any approaches that can offer long-term evidence of effectiveness. I also do not discount patients' power of belief that their diet works, even if it includes elements that are in stark contrast with my own belief system. Take doctor Walter Kempner's rice diet, for example. Known to cure droves of patients from a number of debilitating chronic conditions, the diet contains a ton of sugar, even white sugar. By the accounts of thousands of people, it cured everything from heart disease, to diabetes and cancer. This diet contains everything I advise patients against, yet here it is.

    My personal belief system has undergone many changes and it remains in a state of constant evolution, as I claim no right of supreme ownership to any of my current ideas. That does not mean that I hold no convictions. It simply means that I don't assign self-importance to the degree of stopping to learn and evolve. I am also very much aware of my cognitive filter -- the biased lense we all have when it comes to our convictions.

    I was born in Thracian Bulgaria -- the land of ancient traditions, spirit folklore and mysticism. When anyone was sick or injured, people reached for teas, herbal poultices, rabbit fat or infused grappa before anything else. Everything had a spirit or was an entity of some sort. Expressions such as "you can't kill the spirit of alcoholism, you can only weaken it", "let's appease

Grandma Measles, your cough or what-have-you", and "spicy foods chase sickness away" were the norm. Sickness and conditions were seen as spirits and the words used to describe them treated them like people. People baked honey cakes as offerings for Grandma Measles, kids threw their baby teeth on terracotta roofs as spells for minerally strong adult teeth, and everyone wore interwoven white and red yarn come spring, as rituals seeking health and "rosy cheeks," as the color combination of the yarn.

    My great-grandmother (my maternal grandfather's mother) was an energy worker. Of course that is a newfangled term. She was a "baiachka". She healed people with "baene," roughly translated as incantations or sang prayers. I regret having spent my childhood rolling my eyes at her every time she chanted or dropped oil in a bowl of water as a healing ritual. Waving her arms and praying intently, she was "willing" a favorable outcome, she said. The will was everything. As a modern, progressive young lady, I thought all of this was hogwash. Science was the way to go.

Eventually, I followed up my beliefs by spending twelve years in quantitative research at an advertising analytics firm. That experience brought on additional insights, which once again turned my belief system upside down. Beyond questionnaire bias, research has a number of moving parts, expectations, difficulty in data analysis, and improper representation of the sample population. I do believe in it, it's just not an objective as I once thought.

I still discredit small samples and industry sponsorship immediately. Ancient healing traditions on the other hand, have moved closer to my heart, not only because I was touched by the gratitude of the people my grandmother had healed naturally, but also because quantum theory gives us a scientific basis. In fact, the reason why I am willing to accept quantum medicine is because I am not willing to accept the randomness of miracles.

And science and specifically quantum physics today are pure magic. Surrounded by dogma and being ridiculed into obscurity by outright denial, quantum experiments are being called heresy, as if that work even belongs in the scientific jargon. Anyone familiar with the work of Rupert Sheldrake would agree. What Cayce called Akasha holds elements of what Sheldrake describes as the morphic field -- the world of the unseen, where all memory and information is stored and shared via morphic resonance. As a mainstream scientist, Sheldrake is detested, even abhorred. Nonetheless, he boasts impressive credentials (Cambridge Doctor of Biochemistry, cell biology authority, Harvard-educated historian and philosopher, etc, etc…), and offers continually reaffirmed experimental data:

"There is a lot of circumstantial evidence for morphic resonance. The most striking experiment involved a long series of tests on rat learning that started in Harvard in the 1920s and continued over several decades. Rats learned to escape from a water-maze and subsequent generations learned faster and faster. At the time this looked like an example of Lamarckian inheritance, which was taboo. The interesting thing is that after the rats had learned to escape more than 10 times quicker at Harvard, when rats were tested in Edinburgh, Scotland and in Melbourne, Australia they started more or less where the Harvard rats left off. In Melbourne the rats continued to improve after repeated testing, and this effect was not confined to the descendants of trained rats, suggesting a morphic resonance rather than epigenetic effect. I discuss this evidence in *A New Science of Life*, now in its third edition, called *Morphic Resonance* in the US." (Horgan 2014)

Socio-economic factors and emphasis on sympathetic nervous system activation

Ever wonder where the term "rat race" comes from? The origin of the term maybe unknown or long forgotten, but its connotation is unmistakable. The rat race takes place in corporate America amid sales kickoff events, boardroom meetings, new account contests, quotas, key performance indicators and milestone evaluations. The tone is also unmistakable. It's one of go, hurry, submit, worry, stress! Often accompanied by long hours, forfeited vacation time and lack of sleep, rewards are given for overexhaustion. Burnout is rampant, misery -- en masse. There is no time for travel, creativity, renewal or leisure. Even if vacations are enforced, working from home and being involved in the process and work is still the norm. There is no balance. Yet, Mental Health America (MHA) says that work-like balance is an attainable goal.

To prove a point, in September of 2016, Amazon initiated a program allowing some of its workers to work just 30 hours per week. They received 75% of their normal compensation and retained full benefits. This was done in order to gauge productivity as compared to a 40-hour work week. As expected, the results showed that a person can concentrate only for four or five hours at a time before showing signs of fatigue. Performanced waned after that time.

Turns out everyone suffers when people are being treated like human capital with disregard for biological recharging needs. Companies too. The recent trend toward yoga at the workplace is well received and timely. According to the Huffington Post, the benefits extend into workers' health, as "the International Labor Organization has estimated that roughly ⅓ of all work-related disorders are due to stress, and that the loss caused by such stress-induced disorders amounted 6.6 billion dollars in the U.S."

The article continues to reference office morale and additional health benefits such as blood flow and fluid circulation to joint, spine and brain tissues. Since these fluids are responsible for transporting oxygen and nutrients, removing wastes, and circulating hormones, the author surmises that brain fog could be avoided. Taking short breaks during the day to practice movement and meditation, clears the mind and possibly undoes a lot of the damage that comes from sitting.

Stress and its effect on our bodies

Stress has a profound effect on our wellbeing, and yet enabled by societal expectations, the excuses are all there to spiral us down into a professional-pride abyss, as we pull out an appraisal evaluation out of an overworked hat. Did you know that the US is the most overworked developed nation in the world? We don't rest, we don't turn off our phones, we don't take our vacation days. We don't notice that we are taking years off of our lives and we don't make changes until our cholesterol levels reach dangerous limits or the sleepless nights take additional toll on our high-strung psyche. An article published in 20 Something Finance compares us to our peers around the world.

"According to the Center for American Progress on the topic of work and family life balance, 'in 1960, only 20 percent of mothers worked. Today, 70 percent of American children live in households where all adults are employed.' I don't care who stays home and who works in terms of gender (work opportunity equality for all – it's a family choice). Either way, when all adults are working (single or with a partner), that's a huge hit to the American family and free-time in the American household. The U.S. is the ONLY country in the Americas without a national paid parental leave benefit. The average is over 12 weeks of paid leave anywhere other than Europe and over 20 weeks in Europe. Zero industrialized nations are without a mandatory option for new parents to take parental leave. That is, except for the United States."

In addition, 134 countries have maximum-length-of-work laws, which are absent in the US. 85.8 percent of males and 66.5 percent of females work more than 40 hours per week and we work "137 more hours per year than Japanese workers, 260 more hours per year than British workers, and 499 more hours per year than French workers."

The American paid vacation time and sick time off also need improvement, as there are no laws requiring paid sick days off. The US is the only industrialized nation that does not have a legally mandated annual leave. France and Finland get a fully paid month off each year.

And we need to get back into the realm of personal responsibility. That, for some may not occur naturally unless our health begins to suffer. Awareness is key. Prevention is the single most important factor when it comes to general health and quality of life. And it doesn't have to be complicated. Once our health has been impacted, correction requires time, consistency and effort. Prevention is a sterile word, but it holds joy for life, serenity and bliss. Honoring the cycles of human nature brings rewards. It balances out the stresses in our dailiness.

Parasympathetic response is the counterpart of excessive worry, the great healer of anxious minds. There is an innate familiarity with its importance, yet evoking parasympathetic response requires a new way of thinking. It needs a new hero and a new story. We need to emulate people like Richard Branson, one of the greatest business minds of our time, not only for his entrepreneurial acumen and hard work, but also for his *joie de vivre*. We need to start looking at enjoyment as self-care, as well as caring for those around us, as we become calmer, happier and healthier moms, dads, friends, colleagues and partners.

The guilt surrounding money spent on a vacation or a spa visit has to be replaced with pride similar to the accomplishment we feel after training for a 5K. If the health benefits are similar, why do we praise one and shun the other? Worse yet, why do we label rejuvenation spas as discretionary spending? Some people call self-care a reward, but even that definition exemplifies an unhealthy relationship with relaxation. Americans as a whole have an unhealthy relationship with relaxation and we must change that in order to achieve a shift. Insurance coverage for biofeedback, massage, reflexology, hypnotherapy, yoga, balneotherapy, light and sound therapy, facial rejuvenation, reiki and other holistic modalities may be a good place to begin, because excessive work comes with a steep price. Stress is a primary cause of both mental and physical problems.

The importance of parasympathetic care

The world made a leap forward in the 70s when a well-researched book, authored by Dr. Herbert Benson, a Harvard trained physician, and Miriam Z. Klipper was published. That book is called the Relaxation Response. The material draws on the parasympathetic response, which counters the fight-or-flight response first described in the 1920s by Walter Bradford Cannon. Benson asserts that "more than 60 percent of all visits to healthcare providers are related to stress," as it causes the epinephrine and norepinephrine to be secreted into the bloodstream. The effects that follow include high blood pressure (hypertension), headaches, chronic lower back pain, insomnia, irritable bowel syndrome, heart disease, stroke and even cancer. Further investigation of Dr. Benson's work not only supports his findings, it adds an array of additional benefits from immune system support to anti-inflammatory responses.

The parasympathetic system is responsible for relaxation, healing and digestion. Often referred to as the "rest and digest" system, it is mostly controlled by cranial nerve X, the vagus nerve, and is mainly responsible for body's maintenance. It counters the sympathetic response or the fight-or-flight system, which mobilizes the body during activity. The parasympathetic system is also called the craniosacral system. It consists of preganglionic fibers that start at the brainstem and the sacral part of the spine. The sympathetic system also enables the body to respond to fear. Characterized by deeper breathing, dilated pupils, and cold sweaty skin, the sympathetic system responses help us hunt, work and survive. Unless productively counterbalanced, the stress hormones would actively poison the body with inflammation. Cortisol, for example, is a hormone released into the bloodstream to help the body cope with pressure. After the body secretes adrenaline (epinephrine) as a response to agitation, the heart rate is increased, elevating blood pressure and energy supplies. Cortisol is the hormone that increases glucose in the bloodstream to enhance the brain's use of glucose. It triggers self-healing and repair. Acetylcholine is also released. This hormone activates nicotinic acetylcholine receptors on the postganglionic neurons of the sympathetic system enabling release of noradrenaline, also known as norepinephrine.

Cortisol also curbs non-essential functions and when perpetually activated, suppresses the digestive and reproductive systems, and growth. It is the primary stress hormone that controls mood, attitude, ambition and fear. Once the threat passes, adrenaline and cortisol levels should drop to return to their normal baseline levels. Long term, albeit low-level perpetual cortisol activation can cause a slew of health problems including:

- Anxiety and depression
- Insomnia
- Digestive problems
- Headaches
- Heart disease
- High blood pressure
- Irritability
- Weight gain

- Forgetfulness
- Inability to concentrate, etc.

Strokes and hypertension are also linked to chronically elevated cortisol -- the fight or flight hormone secreted by the body to help us cope with stress. In Understanding the Stress Response, Harvard Health Publishing writes that many people are unable to cope with stress. Like an overworked engine, chronic low-level stress adds additional strain to a burdened system. Persistent epinephrine surges lead to high blood pressure, blood vessel damage and elevated risk of strokes and heart attacks. Higher cortisol levels also contribute to the body's energy stores, therefore sustained contribution increases body fat and causes weight gain.

Cortisol is also released into the bloodstream to metabolize insulin, so sugary foods cause stress response circularity -- cortisol causes stress and stress elevates cortisol. Refined sugars (e.g., white bread, pasta, rice, sweet drinks, etc.) elevate cortisol levels -- a process that signals the cells to store fat, especially in the abdominal part of the body. Although marketers take advantage of this science by offering cortisol blocking pills, sustainable results come with awareness and hard work. Magic pill solutions are not recommended.

Other hormones are also closely related to stress. In fact, we must address the body as an interconnected system because the entire network of biochemical and physiological homeostasis suffers when parasympathetic responses are diminished. In addition to cortisol, we have catecholamines, glucocorticoids, growth hormone and prolactin -- all hormones Mother Nature designed to help us cope with stress and adapt to new life circumstances.

Catecholamines are released when the pituitary-adrenal axis is stimulated. Increased blood flow, cardiac output, sodium retention, vasoconstriction, higher glucose levels, bronchiolar dilatation and behavioral activation follow. In other words, the adrenal sympathetic system suffers during occupational stress and this hormone is released to get your body on high alert.

Acute stress also promulgates the rapid release of vasopressin from the hypothalamus. It is a natural occurring substance that controls several functions. In addition to maintaining cellular function, this antidiuretic hormone regulated heart rhythm, internal body temperature, sleepiness, blood volume and proper flow of urine from the kidneys.

Stress hormones can also affect menstrual cycles and the entire reproductive system. Gonadotropin, for example, released by GnRH, is also rationed during a fight-or-flight mode and that is one of the believed causes for changes in the reproductive system. Thyroid function is down-regulated, as T3 and T4 levels decrease during times of stress. Thyroid-stimulating hormone (TSH) secretion decreases too. Metabolic activity suffers and growth hormone levels go up, as insulin may decrease during stress. This process, along with the increase in its counterbalancing hormones can contribute to stress-induced hyperglycemia (excess sugar in the bloodstream). Why does this matter? Because having excess sugar in the bloodstream for extended periods of time can cause a slew of health problems. It's not difficult to see a domino effect of chemicals reeking havoc on the thyroid, adrenals and the entire body. Hyperglycemia can damage the blood vessel tissues that supply blood to internal organs, leading not only to heart disease and stroke, but also to kidney disease, vision and nerve problems.

Drugabuse.com reports that many prescription medications for pain relief are just a highly addictive pill-forms of heroin. Their physical and psychological effects are similar if not the same as heroin. Heroin is a drug derived from opiate alkaloid substances extracted from the opium poppy, while opiate medications are the same thing in synthetic form. Our bodies' endorphin neuropeptides are natural human forms of opioids, albeit synthesized by our glands. They have the same purpose as opiates, to subdue pain and share molecular composition with botanically derived opiates. These pharmaceutical and endogenous substances interact with opioid receptors located throughout different parts of the brain.

Our bodies' chemicals are able to relieve pain upon traumatic injury. Whether natural or synthetic, opioid molecules attach themselves to the same receptors in the brain, which in turn trigger releases of dopamine -- the feel-good chemical that rewards us with an intense feeling of well-being. The irony is that opiates/opioids are actually depressants, which impair respiration and the heart, and may lead (and often do) to coma and death.

Understanding the process of these chemicals should lead to responsible prescriptions and one would surmise, a campaign for natural treatments of pain. Should endorphin release through bodywork, acupuncture, meditation, exercise, good nutrition, and communing with nature and sunshine be the norm?

Drugs stimulate temporary, excessive release of neurotransmitters that the body had previously stored. The body's reserves are straightened and constantly under pressure to resupply. Leaving these miraculous storage tanks running on dry should not make intuitive sense to anyone. These chemicals (specifically endorphins, enkephalins and dynorphins) are responsible for much more than pain relief. These neurotransmitters -- and there are over 20 types of endorphins alone -- act by sending electrical signals through the nervous system. Natural endorphins help mostly with stress and pain (without the drug addiction), but they also regulate appetite, sex drive and immune responses.

The stress reduction and feeling of well-being is what makes us addicted, one would assume. Channeled endorphins for euphoria take away from the other parasympathetic functions by scrapping one's sex drive, appetite and ability to fight off diseases and infections. The addiction is one of the saddest things a person can do to their own body, as the mind would send seemingly "logical" thoughts of denial, excuses or downright sacrifice. The story of Joe -- referenced on anti-drug television commercials, where a desperately addicted worker breaks his own back on purpose to get more opioids -- is not an isolated case. In the United States, every 12 minutes someone dies from opioid overdose.

The cost to the economy is also mind-boggling. Science News citing The Journal of Pain, published by the American Pain Society reports that the yearly cost of chronic pain is as high as $635 billion a year. That number is higher than the annual costs for heart disease, cancer and diabetes. Studies have traced the economic impact of chronic pain and the comprehensive analysis that followed has been eye opening. Researchers at Johns Hopkins University have been compiling healthcare costs, a well as indirect productivity results by noting productivity of people reporting pain compared to healthy, pain-free individuals. There were 20,214 people studied (all over the age of 18), representing 210.7 million US workers. The definition of pain included hindered ability to work, joint pain, arthritis or other painful chronic discomforts. Indirect costs were calculated by subtracting projected healthcare costs of individuals without pain from those of individuals with pain. Incremental costs were calculated by healthcare payers.

As expected, the findings showed that people with moderate pain had expenditures $4,516 higher that someone with no pain and people with severe pain spent $3,210 higher than those with moderate pain, so $7,726 more than individuals with no pain. The average adult healthcare expenditures were $4,475 and with our aging population, these numbers are only expected to go up. One would surmise that since nutrition is so closely related to pain, companies would invest more in programs geared toward reducing pain and inflammation. Joint pain costs $4,048 more to treat, arthritis costs $5,838 and functional disabilities -- $9,680.

Workers with pain miss more days from work. Tallying up this data with the cost of healthcare added up between $560 to $635 billion dollars. Since healthcare costs were between $261 and $300 billion, other major conditions scored higher, however once the researchers added the cost of lost productivity, that added another

$299 to $334 billion. The researchers added that this number is very conservative since the costs of pain for non-civilian and military personnel, people under 18, caregivers and institutionalized people were not accounted for.

Discomfort from pain affects all areas of one's health. It is closely interconnected with one's psyche, immune response and general well-being. Allopathic medicine, although effective, comes with high costs and serious side effects. The solutions are often debilitating, addictive and near-sighted. The focus is on maintenance rather than a cure. The focus is on 'a pill and now' rather than on lifestyle changes and permanence. Medical facilities promote managements and maintenance for chronic pain, and for a good reason -- unless the whole body is brought back to balance -- through an equal combination of nutrition, adequate chemically-unassisted, natural rest, acupuncture, and other natural modalities -- the pain will most likely persist indefinitely.

The biophysics of pain

Before we start a discussion on quantum medicine for pain and inflammation, we must take a look at the physiological processes behind these conditions. Pain is a defence mechanism resulting from tissue damage. It warns us to prevent tissue damage. Since people experience pain differently, sometimes it is difficult to diagnose. It can be chronic or acute, and it is felt by special nerves called nociceptors. These nerves assess tissue damage and carry the information up the spinal cord to the brain. Pain can take on a number of forms and severities.

Inflammation often accompanies pain, as its most common symptoms include redness and swelling. Defined as: "a process by which the body's white blood cells and substances they produce protect us from infection with foreign organisms," inflammation is also physiological defence mechanism.

There is more to pain that meets the eye. In the 1960s, researchers Melzack and Wall proposed the Gate

Control Theory -- and integrative model centering on the interaction between psychosocial and physiological factors. Widely accepted today, this control refers to the *substantia gelatinosa*, which sits in the dorsal horn of the spinal cord, a little lower than the base of the skull. This gatekeeper sifts through "the amount of afferent impulses from the periphery to the transmission cells (T-cells) of the dorsal horn through inhibitory processes at the neuronal level, and thereby controlling the quantity and intensity of the signals to the central nervous system." In addition, higher cortical functions play a role in the subjective experience of pain. Gatchel posits that negative emotions and conditioning such and hopelessness, helplessness and anger augment sensory input and therefore pain. Meditation, on the other hand, "closes the gate," decreasing the perception of pain.

    Pain and inflammation are controlled by quantum biophysics among other things, therefore science must extrapolate that it can be addressed via quantum medicine -- a new branch of medicine and a perceived voodoo-child mystery, which in reality is pure physics based on precise calculations, experimentation and data. In fact, Erwin Schrodinger himself (the father of the science called quantum mechanics and a Nobel Laureate) proposed the living matter at the cellular level is pure quantum mechanics.

With regard to pain, a physics phenomenon called resonance (recognized as sound of vibration) can be applied to enhance electricity or energy. Quantum medicine uses resonance to augment energy in and between cells. This microscopic molecular resonance can be understood in terms of activation at a specific frequency. In other words, energy transfer is enabled between molecules via resonance. As a result, electromagnetic energy fields administered for pain electronically, would enhance subatomic particle movement and induce healing.

Acupuncture

Acupuncture is an ancient Chinese modality of healing, where needles are inserted into specific points of the body through which energy (or chi) is believed to flow into organs, ligaments, and tissues. It is often discounted by allopathic practitioners as placebo that makes patients believe they are being cured, therefore they are. Nonetheless, acupuncture is today covered by insurance in the United States for pain because actuarial tables have found it to be effective and economically viable. In China, acupuncture is a main method of treatment for all types of conditions, as it is based on a holographic model of the universe, in essence on the Hermetic principles of "as above so below," on the Fibonacci sequence of creation.

There is a divine and clear correspondence in creation as the universe is holographic in nature. Minute, small, big...all parts repeat and exist within the whole. There is also resonance or the invocation of a response from the "like." If one sings at a pitch of a specific frequency, if there is a guitar in the room, the corresponding tone will be created by the guitar without anyone touching it. There is a resonance between the octaves, as per the principle of as above, so below. This is similar to our subtle bodies. A harmed energy body will trickle down to disharmony in the physical body. Shedding stored, revisited memories of trauma is essential to bringing the body to balance and subsequently, healing.

Does acupuncture work via quantum principles? The quantum physics of creation and the work of Professor David Bohm, Einstein's protege and renowned quantum physicist at Princeton University, may be indirectly -- some would argue directly -- in agreement with the premise of acupuncture, by providing empirical evidence that supports the holographic nature of the universe. All patterns in the universe repeat within themselves and are profoundly interconnected.

According to Traditional Chinese Medicine (TCM), there are 12 primary meridians through which energy, also called chi or qi, runs -- heart, pericardium, lung, spleen, liver, kidney, small intestine, large intestine, triple energizer, stomach, gallbladder and bladder.

The heart meridian does not go to the face directly, but through the heart divergent channel through the throat, as it continues up onto the front of the face, until it reaches the bottom inside of the eye next to spot between the eye and the nose, where it connects with the Small Intestine meridian.

The stomach divergent channel is also important because the stomach is so closely related to pain. From the heart, this channel goes upwards until it reaches the throat, the forehead and then back down through the eye, where it ends at acupoint ST1, which is the primary meridian.

The Triple Energizer Meridian treats certain types of headaches and it runs through the scalp and around the ear.

There are also two major extraordinary (sometimes called marvelous) vessels on the head -- the Conception Vessel, with points on the face indicated for mental problems and facial puffiness and the Governing Vessel with its head points often used to treat headaches, anxiety and insomnia.

According to TCM, these acupuncture meridians travel along 12 main channels of the body and are connected to a source of nonlocality. The meridians are extremely sensitive and enable a complex network of communication within the body. Each meridian is connected to a major organ, which is also connected to an emotion.

- Joy -- heart
- Anger -- stomach, liver and spleen
- Anxiety -- lung and large intestine

- Pensiveness -- spleen
- Grief -- lungs
- Fear -- kidneys
- Freight -- heart and kidneys

Needle-free acupuncture

Auriculotherapy a branch of acupuncture that uses points on the ear to help mostly pain, anxiety and addiction withdrawal symptoms. Its benefits, though controversial, are undisputed. Used by hoards of "barefoot physicians" in China (that is what they call themselves), the United States military for battlefield applications, and the Lincoln Hospital in NYC for heroin addiction, auriculotherapy offers a viable, drug-free alternatives for pain, anxiety and addition.

An article published by the US National Library of Medicine, Auricular Neuromodulation: The Emerging Concept beyond the Stimulation of Vagus and Trigeminal Nerves, detail studies done on cadavers by Peuker and Filler (2002), detail anatomo-physiological data, that shows neuromodulation strategies of central nervous system areas considered to be "crucial in the physiopathology of several disorders." In this sense, The external ear, the authors believe, could be "one of the most accurate and powerful at hand tool for brain neuromodulation." (Mercante, Deriu, Ragnon 2018)

In the same article, other experimental research found that stimulation of the area of the auricular concha part of the ear activates the cholinergic anti-inflammatory pathway. It also down-regulates proinflammatory cytokine expressions, hence inhibiting the systemic inflammatory response to endotoxins.

Moreover, the US National Library of Medicine's data supports auriculotherapy and specifically electro-stimulation of the ear with more definitive research and positive scientific conclusions than acupuncture. Studies used by Dolphin MPS (Microcurrent Point Stimulation) also demonstrate how needle-free electroacupuncture effectively stacks up to needles. Needles require 30-45 minutes of a time span for the *chi* to be properly activated. Electro stimulation on the other hand, requires 30 seconds per point. The device is portable and just as effective as acupuncture for many conditions. For some, it has been proven to be even more effective, as measured by increases in heart rate variability (HRV), a key measurement tool in determining pain.

An article published in LiveScience, details results of studies showing that acupuncture and acupressure reduced nausea when the right points were stimulated. It seems, whether real or simulated, acupuncture works. Some physicians feel that acupuncture works based on the placebo effect. Anna Enblom, lead author of a study at the Osher Centre for Integrative Medicine at the Karolinska Institute in Sweden, feels that the benefits come for patients' belief that the treatment works. Karen Sherman, on the other hand, after co-authoring a paper on sham acupuncture suggests that "a non-penetrating needle is only a placebo if the 'active ingredient' is skin penetration." From that regard, she does not believe that these can determine if acupuncture works via the placebo effect.

Phototherapy science and research

Phototherapy is low level laser technology (LLLT) used to treat a number of conditions, from pain and inflammation, to restoration, regeneration and improved function. Photons of light are absorbed by the mitochondrial chromophores of the epidermis, which leads to electron transport, increased blood circulation, adenosine triphosphate (ATP) nitric oxide release, and oxygenation. The diverse signaling pathways get activated. Stem cells are also activated via phototherapy and that in turn leads to healing and tissue repair.

A 583 nm diode is placed over the area of concern as well as the ears and the parietal lobe (the part of the brain that deals with pain interpretation), while the hands are massaged and the vagus nerve is stimulated through gentle reflexology. The selection of these yellow-amber cold laser frequencies was based on decades of anti-inflammatory use. Extensive rheumatoid arthritis studies confirm the findings.

A paper titled Anti-Inflammatory Activities of Light Emitting Diode Irradiation on Collagen-Induced Arthritis in Mice (a secondary publication) details studies that showed how LEDs with wavelengths of 570 nm and 940 mn helped rheumatoid arthritis in mice. Citing other articles in PMC, US National Library of Medicine, this paper was the work of researchers Noboru Kuboyama, Mitsuhiro Ohta, Yusuke Sato and Yoshimitsu Abiko. Credit was also given to the Department of Pharmacology, Nihon University School of Dentistry at Matsudo, the Department of Oral Diagnosis, Nihon University School of Dentistry at Matsudo, the Department of Biochemistry and Molecular Biology, Nihon University School of Dentistry at Matsudo, and the Research Institute of Oral Science, Nihon University School of Dentistry at Matsudo.

These findings show promise, as RA is a common autoimmune disorder that affects joint health in millions of Americans. A total of 20 mice were given collagen stimulated arthritis (CIA) induced by bovine (cow) type II collagen injections. The mice were then subdivided in 4 groups -- control group, CIA group and two groups of LED irradiated CIA mice. The frequencies used were 570 mn (yellow) and 940 nm (red). The mice were treated 3 times per week for 500 seconds per session.

Results determined that in the LED-570 and LED-940 groups, four weeks after arthritis induction, swelling subsided to 18.1±4.9 and 29.3±4.0 respectively with interleukin and MMP-3 serum levels (immunological responses) significantly lower in the LED-940 group.

Conclusions showed that LED phototherapy, particularly in the near-infrared spectrum was effective for inhibition of the inflammatory reactions caused by RA. Researchers felt that the 940 nm wavelength may have a high affinity for living tissue and be capable of inducing biological reactions.

The study also noted that the efficacy of light emitting diodes (LED) for increased circulation, help with post-inflammatory hyperpigmentation (skin darkening), dermatitis, wound healing and mitochondrial activity has also been reported. Collagen-induced Achilles tendonitis was also helped via LED phototherapy with wavelengths of 880 nm, irradiation time 170 s, after only two weeks.

Research points to evidence that every color has a different benefit. Narrow band blue light, for example, (420 nm) has demonstrated safety and efficacy in the treatment of acne. Blue light exhibits a phototoxic effect on Propionibacterium acne too and earlier research found improvement in inflammatory lesions. Since cytokines have demonstrated a vital role in the development of inflammation, IL-1alpha and ICAM-1 were studied as markers. UVB radiation was also brought in and was found to modulate an immune response.

The results were compelling as blue light combined with a low-dose UVB light resulted in "inhibition of cytokine-induced production of IL-1alpha. The level of IL-1alpha decreased by 82% in HaCaT and by 75% in hTERT cells when exposed to blue light. It decreased by 95% in HaCaT and by 91% in hTERT cells when blue light was used in combination with UVB. ICAM-1 expression was similarly reduced in HaCaT, but not in hTERT cells."

In other words, narrow-band blue light was found to subside inflammation, thus expanding the properties of 420 nm to a number of inflammatory processes that go beyond acne and skin conditions.

Green phototherapy has showed promising treatment results for pain as well. Well established to aid with hyperpigmentation (age spots, freckles and other darkening of the skin), green light has been found effective to treat neurological pain. A study by researchers at the University of Arizona concluded that rats with neuropathic pain showed higher tolerance for thermal and tactile stimulus. This may have astonishing applications for people with fibromyalgia as well, although, even with light, we would only be addressing the symptoms, not the causes of the affliction.

An article, Treatment of Pain Gets the Green Light by Robin Tricoles for the Arizona University Communications publication, describes the work of Dr.

Mohab Ibrahim, director of the Comprehensive Pain Management Clinic at Banner-University Medical Center South and Dr. Rajesh Khanna, UA associate professor of pharmacology and senior author of the study.

The idea for the study was prompted by Dr. Ibrahim's brother who would sit in the park, among trees each time he had to deal with his debilitating migraines. Doctor Ibrahim considered tree chemicals being released, serenity or maybe even the calming effects of the greenery around as contributing factors. He decided to study the effects of green phototherapy on chronic pain, as it was not difficult or costly to organize.

A group of rats were placed under plastic containers with attached green LED strips to make sure they are fully submerged in green light. A second group just had contact lenses that allowed the green spectrum wavelength to pass through the lenses. A third group had opaque contact lenses, which blocked green light from entering the eyes.

Upon completion of the study, the first two groups were found to exhibit increased tolerance to both thermal and tactile stimulus revealing benefit for neuropathic pain. The benefits also lasted for four days. No tolerance to the therapy was recorded. To extent the study, the researchers engaged human participants with fibromyalgia. They were given green LED light strips to use in a darkened room every night for an hour or two. The study continued for 10 weeks with great results. A couple of the participants never returned because their pain had been helped and one wrote to Dr. Ibrahim to request that the green light is returned to him. The therapy worked well for both males and females and was celebrated by many seeking side-effect free, non-pharmacological methods for treating chronic pain.

This study was also discussed in Fibromyalgia News Today, a publication geared toward fibromyalgia sufferers and healers. Supporting the general thesis of neurotransmitters' role in regulating pain, this publication periodically publishes neurotransmitter studies on the subject as well.

Experimentally proven observations are convincing, especially when it comes to seeking respite from pain, and the scientific mechanisms through which they work are extraordinary. Unfortunately, they don't come without limitations. Exact distance, frequency and duration may or may not matter, yet we have an idea that cellular photobiostimulation appears to have a wide range of effects at the molecular, cellular, and tissue levels.

Scientists postulate that it may work through absorption of red and near infrared light by mitochondrial chromophores, in particular cytochrome c oxidase (CCO). Photo-acceptors in the plasma membrane of the cells are also considered. A domino effect occurs in the mitochondria, and its effect is believed to lead to biostimulation of a number of processes. Researchers believe that light absorption may cause photodissociation of inhibitory nitric oxide, leading to enzyme activity, electron transport, mitochondrial respiration and adenosine triphosphate (ATP) production. Phototherapy is linked to the activation of intracellular signaling pathways, and it changes the affinity of transcription factors involved with survival, regeneration and tissue repair.

Low level light has limited skin penetration, so its effects on the body should be limited to skin, yet the studies that prove phototherapy effectiveness suggest that it is not. Could light therapy work via meridians? It turns out that acupuncture meridians do facilitate the body's absorption of light. Russian researchers were able to track light in the body by magnifying it with an apparatus called a photomultiplier. Only some parts of the body were able to transfer light beneath the surface, and they corresponded to acupuncture points. The light was further conducted along the acupuncture meridians. Deeper physiological processes were influenced. The transmission of photons, travelling at the speed of light within the meridian system, may be a more fundamental (and closer to physics) aspect of Chi/Qi/Prana/Vital force workings.

In addition, the effectiveness of light and electricity as means of acupuncture meridian stimulation is not difficult to grasp in terms of physics, as matter is a function of light. Humans are deeply connected to the speed with which light travels from our sun. We are in fact, light beings because our energetic signature is nothing more than our mass multiplied by the speed of light squared. Einstein's equation, $E=mc^2$ applies to all. Our mass is nothing more than energy divided by the speed of light squared ($m=E/c^2$). Are we then just slowed down light?

    This is perhaps the reason why using light and/or electricity is just as effective as using metal needles. In fact, today we have no evidence that metal needles were used in ancient China. Evidence does suggest, however, that the first emperor of China had electricity. Could the ancient Chinese have used it for healing purposes?

The vagus nerve

The vagus nerve is central in parasympathetic response, as it balances the nervous system acting as the relaxed partner of the sympathetic (fight-or-flight) response. It runs along the entire spine, from the base of the skull to the tailbone. The vagus nerve is in charge of the digestive tract, heart rate, blood pressure, breathing, urination and sexual arousal. According to Medical News Today, the nerve enables the mind-gut connection, relaxes the body, lowers blood pressure, relieves fears and helps our bodies deal with inflammation.

Electrical stimulation of the vagus nerve has been used in allopathic medicine for decades. Clinical trials paved the way for epilepsy treatments via vagus nerve stimulation in 1997, and later in 2005, the FDA approved it as a treatment for depression. Since the vagus nerve had connections to almost all internal organs, it is not a stretch for scientists to postulate that other conditions may be helped by vagus nerve stimulation as well.

Medical News Today discusses a 2016 study that shows how the vagus nerve stimulation can help patients with rheumatoid arthritis. A study published at the US National Library of Medicine also concludes that vagus nerve stimulation attenuates systemic inflammatory responses. Conducted by Borovikova LV1, Ivanova S, Zhang M, Yang H, Botchkina GI, Watkins LR, Wang H, Abumrad N, Eaton JW, Tracey KJ at the Picower Institute for Medical Research in NY, the study focused on endotoxin prompted inflammation and bodily response via anti-inflammatory pathways. As expected, the afferent nerve fibres were activated, but this particular research found an unrecognized, parasympathetic anti-inflammatory pathway that enabled the brain to subdue the inflammation via vagus nerve stimulation. The study concluded that vagus nerve stimulation attenuates the systemic inflammatory response to endotoxins.

Ultrasound gua sha

Another modality for pain includes the use of ultrasound gua sha. This treatment combines Traditional Chinese Medicine and sound technology. Gua sha is an ancient technique that roughly translates into scraping. It has been used to increase circulation and improve stagnation.

A study published by Dr. Arya Nielsen, PhD at the Pacific College of Oriental Medicine asserts that gua sha increases surface microperfusion (blood circulation). In the study, 11 doctors and nurses with muscle pain had gua sha done, after which they were scanned with laser Doppler Imaging. Researchers found 400% increase in microperfusion (blood circulation) for 7.5 minutes right after each treatment and a statistically significant improvement for full 25 minutes after.

Dr. Nielsen also describes an astonishing 2009 study done at Harvard showing that gua sha upregulated gene expression for protective enzymes (heme oxygenase-1), "at multiple internal organ sites immediately after treatment and over a period of days following gua sha treatment." This enzyme also regulates asthma, IBS, and organ transplant rejection, and inflammation. It is evident why this ancient modality has been used for pain, internal organ stimulation and inflammation for millenia.

The combination with ultrasound has been beneficial and supported by research. A survey of therapeutic ultrasound use by physical therapists authored by Wong RA, Schumann B, Townsend R, Phelps CA at the Department of Physical Therapy of Marymount University, examined the opinions of physical therapists. 457 physical therapists were invited to share their perceived clinical importance of ultrasound for common orthopedic issues. The response rate was 45.3%. 83.6% PTs stated that they were likely to use ultrasound as a healing method to decrease soft tissue inflammation for conditions such as tendinitis and bursitis. 70.9% of PTs would use the device to increase tissue extensibility, 54.1% for soft tissue inflammation, 49.3% for pain reduction and 35.1% to reduce swelling.

High frequency

Developed by Nikola Tesla, high frequency is an important tool for many practitioners. According to Wikipedia, the Tesla Ray is an antique medical device, electrotherapy that delivers high frequency and low current for therapeutic purposes. The device was said to cure just about everything -- from cancer to skin conditions. I works by adding electrons to atoms. The transfer of electrons from any source neutralizes free radicals. Since inflammation is caused by free radicals and electrons are the source of the neutralizing power of antioxidants, high frequency therapy should be effective in treating pain and inflammation.

High frequency alternative practitioners have been persecuted and denounced for years. Today, high frequency treatments are gaining momentum and even insurance companies recommend them prior to knee replacement surgeries.

Most facial spas in the United States use the Tesla Ray on the face. Used for over a 100 years as an anti-aging treatment, the Tesla Ray, also called violet ray or high frequency wand, is known to help with acne, eye puffiness, large pores, dark circles, fine lines and wrinkles and skin rejuvenation. High frequency treatments stimulate cell regeneration, oxygenation, blood circulation and product penetration. They have been shown to eliminate toxins, encourage lymphatic drainage and increase collagen and elastin production.

Violet ray treatments were said to cure everything from lumbago to carbuncles. From an antique Master Violet Ray manual c. 1920 comes this treatment advice:

"Brain Fog - Use Applicator No. I over forehead and eyes. Also treat the back of head and neck with strong current in direct contact with the skin. Treat the spine and hold the electrode in the hand. Ozone inhalations for about four minutes are also of importance." (Langford 2008)

Recent therapeutic acceptance of high frequency treatments needs to be noted. Dr. Christopher Winfree, a neurosurgeon at the Columbia University Medical Center/NewYork-Presbyterian Hospital, uses high frequency stimulation to help patients with chronic pain. An article published by the Neurological Institute of NY describes patients nerves as "messengers, carrying information to and from the brain. When damaged, these nerves can get stuck repeating a signal over and over. When that signal is pain, and it continues uninterrupted for more than three months, physicians define it as a chronic pain condition."

Dr. Winfree considers spinal cord stimulation (any type, not just high frequency) a viable option for those facing surgery. His method includes implanting electrodes near the spine and he has found these treatments to be highly effective, taking his message on the road by speaking at conferences around the world.

Additional research supports his findings and many, many medical doctors and neurosurgeons offer high frequency treatments all over the United States. An article in Science Daily titled High-Frequency Spinal Cord Stimulation Provides Better Results in Chronic Back, Leg Pain, offers empirical data. A high-frequency spinal cord stimulation (SCS) technique is discussed as a treatment with superior clinical outcomes, compared to conventional low-frequency SCS. Clinical trials in the November issue of *Neurosurgery*, describes the 'HF10' technique as a treatment offering lasting reductions in back and leg pain after other treatments have failed.

The featured study included 171 patients. "At three months, scores for back and leg pain decreased by at least half in more than 80 percent of patients receiving HF10. By comparison, conventional SCS achieved similar responses in back pain for 44 percent of patients and in leg pain for 55 percent."

Not only was this high frequency treatment highly effective, the article continues to describe patients' two-year follow-up. The results again showed 76 versus 49 percent improvement for back pain and 73 versus 49 percent improvement for leg pain. Dr. Kapural, a featured physician in the article, finds these treatments impressive and believes they may be useful for arm and neck pain as well. He and his colleagues conclude: "The superior and durable results demonstrated in this study are anticipated to lead to improved long-term cost effectiveness and payer acceptance, making this therapy broadly available to patients suffering from chronic pain."

Current uses of the Tesla ray include: pain management, improvement of blood flow, range of joint movement, strength, muscle stimulation, tissue repair, edema (inflammation), hair regrowth and skin rejuvenation.

It must also be noted that the persecution of high frequency practitioners when it comes to cancer cures may have been unwarranted. Although allopathic medicine should not be replaced or ignored, a study by the Division of Hematology and Oncology at the University of Alabama, has found that radiofrequency electromagnetic fields amplitude-modulated at tumor-specific frequencies are effective for targeted treatment of cancer. Since this is not relevant to my thesis, I will not go into detail. My assertion is that radio frequency waves stimulate blood flow and oxygenation, and that aspect of these frequencies is widely-accepted today.

Nutrition and its effects on biological processes

The power of nutrition cannot be overstated when it comes to treating pain. The process of ingesting food for energy, growth, metabolism, and repair is vast in scope and implications. Besides the obvious -- that we cannot live without it -- the stages of digestion, absorption, transport, assimilation, and excretion flood the organism with possibilities. These possibilities include systemic irregularities, a clean biological mechanism or a little bit of both. The truth is, nutrition plays a central role in our dailiness, not just as a source of sustenance but also as a biochemical supply factory for healing, feeling, glowing, and growing. Depending on the quality of nutrients one ingests, the opposite is also true. The food we eat can make us sick, sad and drab. Mindfulness matters.

One of the immediate effects of food is on hormonal balance. The obvious causes of hormonal fluctuations include stress, poor gut health, certain medications, exposure to toxins, lack of sleep, and unhealthy lifestyle choices (e.g., smoking, drinking, sedentarism, excess caffeine, not getting enough sun and vitamin D, drug use, etc.). All of the above promote inflammation. In oversimplified terms, these activities either import or stimulate the secretion of toxic chemicals that the body combats by sending "firefighters" to put out the fire with water. The Merriam-Webster dictionary defines inflammation as "a local response to cellular injury that is marked by capillary dilatation, leukocytic infiltration, redness, heat, pain, swelling, and often loss of function and that serves as a mechanism initiating the elimination of noxious agents and of damaged tissue."

Common inflammatory foods include processed foods, refined sugars, dairy, GMO and pesticide-laden crops, and animal protein. Although the majority of the population is already aware of these facts, there are also vast amounts of misinformation, special interests and industry-sponsored studies. A few of us stop to think about why processed foods would be bad for us. Obviously, these foods have synthetic chemicals and preservatives, but some kind of preservation has been practiced for millenia. Southern climates have been over-spicing, over-salting and pickling since the beginning of time. How is all of that different today? Today, we use things like aspartame, sulfur dioxide, potassium bromate, monosodium glutamate (MSG), synthetic food dyes, trans fats, sodium sulfite, sodium nitrate and nitrite, as well as BHA and BHT, all raising serious health concerns.

In addition, we need to stop removing nutrients and leaving our foods whole. I will point at fiber, but the examples are numerous. When fiber is removed, so are the many minerals that alkalize the body and offset the acidic byproduct of starches. We find ourselves consuming white breads and pastas, void of minerals and laced with chemicals. Candida overgrowth becomes a problem as an opportunistic scavenger comforted in a hospitable environment since our good microbes have been additionally suppressed by pesticides and herbicides. Candida spores are extremely resilient, surviving toxic substances and thriving in an acidic environment. Alcohol consumption kills beneficial bacteria, but candida bounces back and permeates the whole body through a newly compromised leaky gut. Consequently, foods that feed candida also promote inflammation.

And according to a study featured in Science Daily, inflammation is also linked to chronic pain. A research paper titled: Inflammation Linked To Chronic Pain: Study (ScienceDaily, 7 December 2005) postulates that elevated levels of a protein responsible for persistent pain (NR2B), cause the brain to mimic that pain long after source has disappeared. Professors Min Zhuo and Michael Smith "believe that the body's inflammatory response helps to etch the initial pain into our memory."

During the study, mice were injected with an irritant that caused inflammation. Brain activity in the part of the brain associated with pain was measured one, six and twenty-four hours after each injection. Researchers found NR2B protein levels had increased, indicating an obvious link between memory and pain. These findings have significant pharmacological implications since current medications block all receptors – not just NR2B receptors. Since pain has a vital warning purpose, honing in one one specific receptor would be preferred.

While pharmacology seeks to mitigate symptoms, natural medicine fosters a different approach -- one that targets the source of the inflammation. Sometimes that is not achievable, but often times it is. All we need to do is practice mindfulness, patience and discipline when it comes to the factors we can control. Mindful shopping, cooking and exposure go a long way. Fresh, live food jam-packed with salubrious enzymes and amino-acids should comprise the bulk of most diets.

Chronic inflammation is also linked to heart disease and rheumatoid arthritis. Specifically, many people with rheumatoid arthritis have been found to have chronic inflammation in the heart called sarcoidosis. Researchers at Columbia University in New York City have done numerous studies aiming to improve the heart by mitigating arthritis symptoms. An important outcome of the study was the fact that increased arthritis treatment did indeed lower the levels of inflammation in the heart.

We cannot discuss inflammation and heart disease without presenting the overwhelming data in support of a whole-food plant-based diet. The NY Times hailed Dr. T. Colin Campbell's book The China Study: The Most Comprehensive Study on Nutrition Ever Conducted and the Startling Implications for Diet, Weight Loss, and Long-Term Health as the "Grand Prix of Epidemiology" (2005). Extensive research and meticulously controlled studies found that certain diseases, such as cancer, heart disease and diabetes (dubbed as diseases of affluence) may be attributed to nutritional indulgence. Detailed analyses concluded that "overall, the closer people came to an all plant-based diet, the lower their risk for chronic disease." (Campbell 2017)

In The China Study, Dr. Campbell eloquently furnishes vast amounts of data and evidence from nutrition studies at Blue Zones -- areas of the world with high longevity rates and not coincidentally, predominantly plant-based diets. Dr. Campbell goes on to present study after study on the healthful effects of animal protein-void foods followed by experimentation, where cancer genes become expressed in the presence of casein (animal protein found in milk) and suppressed through exclusive plant material consumption. Indisputable historical data, showing sharp chronic disease declines in the absence of animal protein, are also presented.

The mind-gut connection

Parasympathetic response is unequivocally dependent on nutrition. Pointing at the obvious -- that we cannot adequately relax and, therefore, regenerate at full capacity when we are in pain -- nutrition can provide the biochemical terrain to subside inflammation and evoke parasympathetic response. But the enteric nervous system (the two layers of over 100 million nerve cells lining our gastrointestinal tract) is much more complicated than that. Emotional response often leads to upset stomach, bloating, pain and irritable bowel syndrome (IBS).

The medical community has known about this link for decades. Researchers at Johns Hopkins, however, have evidence of the gut affecting the mind as well. In other words, gastrointestinal irritation may send signals to the central nervous system, which includes the parasympathetic system too. The result? Mood changes. Jay Pasricha, MD who has led this research, postulates that this is why higher-than-normal percentage of people with IBS experience anxiety and depression. Dr. Pasricha also notes that digestive-system activity may have an impact on thinking, memory, metabolism and risks of type 2 diabetes.

The inflammatory or anti-inflammatory effects of nutrition are well documented and widely accepted. Inflammation happens when the body's defence force (white blood cells and other regulating compounds) sends soldiers to capture, engulf or dismantle cellular debris, foreign particles or invading microorganisms, such as viruses, bacteria, foreign organisms, pollution or toxins. In addition to the average American being exposed to thousands of toxins through air, water, soil and chemicals in processed foods, they are also in household cleaners, cosmetics, dyes, glues, solvents, and more. Moreover "of the more than 80,000 chemicals currently used in the United States, most haven't been adequately tested for their effects on human health." (NRDC) To add insult to the injury, we overtax our systems with excessive worry, insomnia, alcohol, other mind-altering substances and overeating as a means of coping with stress.

Consuming fiber, for example, naturally reduces inflammation through the phytonutrients found in plants. Studies suggest the fiber consumption lowers inflammation markers, such as C-reactive protein levels, in the blood of the studies subjects. High CRP levels have been linked to rheumatoid arthritis (RA), diabetes, and heart disease. Whole grains reduce inflammation trifold -- by lowering body weight, by sponsoring a healthy microbiome and by supplying healthy phytonutrients.

Antioxidants fight free radicals. These and other inflammation causing atoms have an odd number of electrons (they are normally paired). Once an atom has lost an electron, it becomes highly reactive and can start a chain reaction of stealing other electrons and breaking up pairs. This process can damage the DNA and the cell membrane. It doesn't always have to cause pain, as internal organs must be severely impaired for pain to take hold. Nonetheless, inflammation may be present.

Antioxidants offer mitigation by scavenging free radicals. Principal substances that do this are vitamins E and C, beta-carotene and selenium.

Cruciferous vegetables such as cabbage, kale, broccoli, Brussels sprouts, bok choy and cauliflower are also excellent anti-inflammatory options. In addition to containing a slew of beneficial vitamins and minerals such as C, B6, A, K, E, manganese, calcium, magnesium and potassium, cruciferous vegetables are also known to fight inflammation. Cabbages gather cadmium-binding substances such as glutamine, a potent anti-inflammatory compound. According to Organic Facts, cabbage consumption "can reduce the effects of many types of inflammation, irritation, allergies, joint pain, fever, and various skin disorders." (Organic Facts 2013)

Foods such as fish, flax meal, walnuts, and legumes such as white, black, navy, kidney beans and soy are rich in Omega-3s. Omega-3 is a polyunsaturated fatty acid. Evidence suggests that (with its consumption) intracellular signaling and gene expression pathways are affected. Clinical studies conclude that omega-3 fatty acids have potent anti-inflammatory properties.

Refined sugars greatly attribute to inflammation. This simple fact may seem self-evident as sugar turns to acid once metabolized. Clinical trials described by Healthline Magazine for example, show that people who were asked to drink soda had increased levels of inflammatory uric acid. Consuming large amounts of fructose also leads to obesity, cancer, diabetes, kidney problems and fatty liver disease. Refined sugar also causes inflammation within the endothelial cells -- specialized epithelial cells found in blood vessels.

Nuts boast amazing nutrients, but they also contain high amounts of phytic acid, which has been linked to poor mineral absorption. To retain the nutrients while shedding the acid, soak in water prior to consumption. Additional enzyme inhibitors, such as polyphenols (tannins), and goitrogens, may also be present. Since digestive enzymes aid food breakdown and nutrient assimilation, neutralizing these substances prior to ingestion is recommended.

Reducing meat and dairy consumption has been linked to helping inflammation. Since inflammation is a protective attack against a threat, scientists felt that threat may have been the animal protein being rejected similarly to a foreign implant. Surprisingly, they discovered that the body rejects whip cream too and that is mostly animal fat. This groundbreaking discovery showed that even a single meat containing animal product flooded one's bloodstream with endotoxins. Endotoxins come from bacteria...from our own gut? The supposition was that animal products cause leaky gut, which in turn allow for gut bacteria to enter our bloodstream. Studies on mice experimentally confirmed that mice do get leaky guts from eating animal products. Except, inflammation after a meal of meat, dairy or eggs started soon after digestion...much sooner than the time needed for the food to reach the large intestine where these potent toxins reside. Endotoxins come from animal products and today we know that foods such as pork, chicken, beef, lamb, eggs and dairy are loaded with them. No matter how much we cook, roast, boil, bake or grill animal flesh, endotoxins live on undisturbed. Animal products cause endotoxemic surge of inflammation.

Pain does great harm to our body's biochemistry and so do synthetic painkillers, therefore, in addition to ending inflammation, we must also address other serious imbalances. During an opioid addiction the neurotransmitters dopamine, serotonin, endorphins, GABA and acetylcholine are depleted even if painkiller use is limited to as little as two weeks.

Although the main natural opioids are endorphins, the other chemicals play vital roles in the body as well. Dopamine is a feel-good hormone that regulates mood, energy and motivation. Serotonin regulates sleep and appetite, GABA is a natural tranquilizer, and acetylcholine helps process information and memory. The longer one uses prescription painkillers, the less neurotransmitters the brain produces. Synthetically induced rewards are also 2 to 10 times stronger.

The dangers are many and they are not to be overlooked, yet we must not discount the merits of science in the area of pain research. When the body suffers and needs relief now, prescription medications have proven to offer unparalleled relief. Many people today cannot function properly without their medications. When a person experiences pain and simple remedies are not working, the use of painkillers may be warranted.

One of those wide-spread conditions, rheumatoid arthritis (RA) is particularly debilitating. It is however an affliction, which responds particularly well to diet. It affects over 1.3 million Americans. Rheumatoid arthritis is more common for women than men and is often found in regions with high animal products consumption. It is a painful condition, which inflames the joints of the body. RA may be an autoimmune response to animal products, particularly to endotoxemia caused by bacteria found in animal products.

Inflammation is also triggered by arachidonic acid, which is an Omega-6 found in animal products. Neu5Gc -- an inflammatory molecule found in human tumors most likely comes from animal product consumption as well. It has been long known that plant-based diets lead to significantly reduced inflammation markers.

Another condition, a disease of endotoxemia and inflammation, is fibromyalgia. Many practitioners consider fibromyalgia a disease of food. Inflammation is always discussed by naturopaths as the root cause of all chronic illness; rheumatoid arthritis and fibromyalgia, specifically, are linked to gut health by allopathic practitioners as well. A limitation of healthcare, however, includes not only coding and reimbursement, it also faces the challenge of the lack of communication between practitioners. Most fibromyalgia treatments are indicative examples of medicine gone awry. Once a disease no one had ever heard of, now fibromyalgia is the norm in people who have been on medication for a while. And allopathic medicine is once again on a quest to treat the symptoms not the causes. Medications focus on blocking pain receptors.

According to WebMD, fibromyalgia is "a glitch in the way your brain and spinal cord handle pain signals." Risk factors include genetic predisposition, gender, arthritis, anxiety, depression, emotional, physical abuse, PTSD, and other stressors. The article does not discuss chemical sensitivities, toxicity and food additives although a link is established. According to Everyday Health Magazine, food additives have been found to be contributing factors. Substances such as aspartame in its various marketed forms, hydrolyzed protein, MSG and other endotoxins over-excite neurotransmitter receptor sites. The article describes two patients losing their fibromyalgia by eliminating aspartame from their diet, although it cautions about the small size of the study. A naturopathic physician also shares his experience with helping patients by eliminating food additives. In a Portland, OR study, patients with fibromyalgia were prescribed an additive-free diet for a month. These patients had both fibromyalgia and IBS. 30% of them experienced a reduction in symptoms. When the food additives were added back to their diets, only 3 days after the patients drank juice with MSG, their symptoms returned. To retain the authenticity of expectation, half of the patients drank placebo juice with no additives. Those patients remained symptom-free.

The above research shows 30% of adults losing their fibromyalgia just by cutting additives out of their diet. How about the other 70%? Turns out endotoxemia is largely caused by animal protein.

A study titled, Fibromyalgia Syndrome Improved Using a Mostly Raw Vegetarian Diet: An Observational Study, was conducted by researchers Michael Donaldson, Neal Speight, and Stephen Loomis at Hallelujah Acres Foundation, Shelby, NC, Center for Wellness, Charlotte, NC and the Cleveland Physical Therapy Associates of Shelby, NC. It followed 30 fibromyalgia patients, who were asked to adopt a raw plant-based diet. 20 subjects remained in the study. 19 of the 20 participants responded very favorably, seeing significant improvement in all fibromyalgia symptoms. Although further testing is warranted due to the small size of this study, the authors concluded that "a diet intervention using a mostly raw, pure vegetarian diet produced dramatic improvements in FMS symptoms." It is important to note that the authors of the study had no competing interests -- financial or otherwise.

Quantum medicine

All of the above suppositions, deductions and conclusions reside within the realm of a fast-growing field called quantum medicine. Humans have been documenting, studying and revering its effects for millennia. In the absence of science, spontaneous healing, even remissions of the most aggressive types of cancers have been contributed to divine intervention or misdiagnosis. Science simply overlooks its existence, although its presence cannot be ignored. Clinical trials call a tiny, spontaneous part of it, the placebo effect. Belief is the part of our story that re-writes our destiny. Born in proven science, quantum medicine charts possibilities, miracles and the future of medicine. Does it lay the ground for quantum (light and sound) technologies, quantum biofeedback, quantum hematology, medical herbalism, bioenergetic dynamism, etc., etc? The world is quite literally in our hands, says Joe Dispenza, Doctor of Chiropractic, neuroscientist, a world renowned author and lecturer at Quantum University.

Although the definitions and use of quantum medicine are being advanced and standardized today, the concept or its workings are not new. Why this field was not developed sooner is not a mystery. Marred by politics, regulations and rigid business modeling, modern medicine still uses Newtonian physics, which is not the best option when we consider the infinitesimally small systems and biochemicals that govern the physiological processes within our bodies. Quantum physics gives us the best modeling of nature in the world of the very small.

It all started in 1900 when physicist Max Planck was studying something called ultraviolet catastrophe -- an incongruence of scientific predictions and what was actually happening. Based on Newtonian physics, if a black box was heated up in such a way that the light could not escape, an infinite amount of ultraviolet radiation should have been produced. That did not occur, but the perceived paradox eventually led to Einstein's supposition that light was made up of particles. These particles were named photons by Gilbert Lewis in 1926. The basic idea was that particles could contain energy of certain sizes led to Niels' Bohr discovery that this energy is not arbitrary and is organized in multiples of standard quantum of energy.

In simple terms, quantum physics is the science of the infinitesimally small and it's a magical, mystery land where two particles can exist in the same space and time, a particle can exist in two places at the same time, it can spin both to the left and to the right simultaneously, and it can change behaviour depending on whether it is being observed or not. And the strangeness does not end there. Reality in itself does not exist until it is being measured. Quantum physics is the world of probability. If an object is given a choice on how to behave, no decision is made until the object is observed.

Much more than a theory, this branch of science is used ubiquitously in modern technology. In one study, a test conducted by Professor Andrew Truscott, used a single helium atom which was isolated, moved through a laser beam, and left to "decide" which way to go. At the same time a random generator was used to decide whether to split the beam to obstruct the atom or not. The atom didn't go from point A to point B. It decided on which way it would go and whether to behave as a particle or as a wave only after it was measured, the research found. This experiment was originally proposed by John Wheeler in 1978, but it was impossible to be run at the time, until the researchers came up with something similar. At the end of the day, the end result confirmed the postulation -- it showed that measurement creates reality ... at least, at the quantum level.

David Bohm also studied wave functions governed by Schrodinger's equation, the math that led to paradoxical quantum uncertainties. Bohm disagreed with the Copenhagen interpretation of Heisenberg's Uncertainty Principle by asserting that every particle has a definite location (even when it's not being observed) and if you know its position, you can determine where it will end up. Unlike in the classical mechanics view, however, Bohm worked from a position of nonlocality. In other words, the supposition of "spooky action at a distance" remains. What that means is that when a cell divides and something is done to that cell, the split off cell would feel it too, no matter the distance. This is called quantum entanglement and hundreds of experiments beginning in the 80s, have proven its existence.

The startling implications of quantum healing assigns power to ordinary people previously reserved for Olympus. Having evidence that points to self-healing as a viable science-backed technique is grand and empowering. It's not an easy-heal button or a pill. It requires a different environment on a macro and micro levels, deep faith, patience and a new awareness of one's condition. It requires fundamental creativity, giving life to a new insight ... or situational creativity -- a new lesson from an old problem. In studying spontaneous remissions, Dr. Amit Goswami (a leading quantum physicist, author, lecturer, thinker, researcher and the author of one of the most successful, globally used quantum mechanics textbooks to date) writes:

> "...scientific materialism leaves no room for theorizing about non-physical sources of human

disease. But is this belief system correct? In fact, it is based on an archaic Newtonian physics that has been replaced by a new paradigm called quantum physics quite some time ago. Quantum objects are transcendent waves of possibility residing in a domain of potentiality; when subjected to measurement, however, they behave as particles in the physical space and time. This is contrary to scientific materialism: not one domain of reality, but two. Quantum physics also allows nonlocality, signalless communication, opening wide the question of nonphysical source of causality."

Dr. Goswami continues to question determinism and thus what modern medicine is based on, as determinism does not hold water based on current scientific advancements. Quantum science is probabilistic and thus casts doubt on genetic determinism. It shows a new approach in integrating conventional and alternative treatment methods supported by non-deterministic measurement, psychophysical parallelism and experimental data.

A wave of possibility becomes a particle of actuality when observed and science lays consciousness as the foundation of all being. As an observer chooses from many possible outcomes within a possibility wave, the observer himself/herself is responsible for the collapse of a wave into a particle. In order for us to do that consciously, we need to understand psychology and in this case, Carl Jung's classifications of experience -- sensing, feeling, thinking and intuiting. Jung's empirical data dismantles scientific materialism; cause and effect flow through human experience. Dr. Goswami builds on these notions by depicting four non-physical "bodies or worlds of quantum possibilities." He names them vital, mental, supramental and bliss.

Quantum medicine deals with all five human bodies, the one physical and four non-physical. Each of these bodies carries a different quality of information. They run from more subtle to more solid, starting with

Bliss and ending with the Physical Body. The quantum balance in a life-form is a prerequisite for healing.

The subtle blueprints for our organs exist in a non-physical realm called morphogenetic fields. Proposed by the previously mentioned Cambridge-educated scientist, Rupert Sheldrake, these fields respond to a phenomenon called morphic resonance. In Sheldrake's own words, "Morphic resonance is the influence of previous structures of activity on subsequent similar structures of activity organized by morphic fields. It enables memories to pass across both space and time from the past. The greater the similarity, the greater the influence of morphic resonance. What this means is that all self-organizing systems, such as molecules, crystals, cells, plants, animals and animal societies, have a collective memory on which each individual draws and to which it contributes."

Quantum medicine aims to restore the morphogenetic field through an integrative approach. Dr.

Paul Drouin, a Canadian medical doctor, acupuncturist, professor, thinker and pro-consciousness author, writes that the purpose of quantum medicine is to "restore the morphogenetic field, the blueprint for the organs, to its full potential, tuning in to a creative mode of operating in relation with the higher self. Positive health is achieved when the physical, vital, mental, supramental, and bliss bodies are in tune and congruent with the core source."

The subtle world of emotions creates tens of thousands of naturally secreted chemicals that rush through our bodies, evoking sympathetic response. The disease-causing role of imbalances has been long known, as the body vigorously labors to achieve homeostasis. What we have ignored is that these chemicals can bring balance as well. Direct look at brain activity while experiencing gratitude, for example, has shown blood flow in various parts of the brain. Overall higher levels of activity in the hypothalamus have also been detected. Since the hypothalamus controls a huge array of essential bodily functions (e.g., drinking, eating, sleeping and metabolism among others), it also affects stress levels. Grateful people were found to be happier and healthier with improved sleep, decreased depression levels and fewer aches and pains.

> "Furthermore, feelings of gratitude directly activated brain regions associated with the neurotransmitter dopamine. Dopamine feels good to get, which is why it's generally considered the "reward" neurotransmitter."
>
> -- Alex Korb, PhD (2012)

The link between our emotions and the chemicals released in our bodies are the basis for vital body medicine, although the vital energy movements of feeling are also aided or deterred by nutrition, as depicted by vital energy traditions of healing such as Traditional Chinese Medicine, homeopathy, and Ayurveda.

> "This scientific validation of our subtle experiences of feeling, thinking, and intuition, opens the door for the validation of alternative practices of

medicine that postulate an important disease-causing role to imbalances of the subtle movements of our experience... now that quantum physics has enabled us, a unified way of incorporating all our experiences within one integral metaphysics, we can also integrate all the medicine practices within one unified practice of quantum integral medicine." (Goswami 2013)

The leap from thoughts to emotions is basic and easy to grasp. This exemplifies transference from the vital body to the physical body. Intuition, or the subconscious picking up of signs and imbalances that are present (although we are not consciously aware) are also not difficult to comprehend. This depicts a flow from the supramental to the mental body of an individual. Bliss is somewhat elusive, yet a logical extennuation of the hierarchy of thought and creation. According to Goswami, riding along the wave of possibility is a path charted by signalless communication stemming from a non-locality. We may choose from particles along the path, but we cannot change the waves of possibility, where a conflicting paradox maybe created. Simply stated, our dreams have a better chance of manifestation if they include selfless thoughts geared toward the betterment of humanity, community, family or children. We are parts of the whole, and that whole seeks out ways to better itself, to self-heal and repair. That is entanglement.

How do we transfer this knowledge further into healing? The fine mastery of quantum healing is related to consciousness, asserts Dr. Paul Drouin, referencing Dr. Deepak Chopra's book, Quantum Healing. One of the observations that gives an insight into the miraculous healings of terminal patients was the realization that the turning point came after the patients had experienced a new awareness of their situation. Dr. Amit Goswami adds the concept of Quantum Creativity to the blueprint of quantum healing.

Dr. Drouin has written extensively on his motivation in laying the groundwork toward a new paradigm in healthcare. His book, Creative Integrative Medicine, foresees a revolution that would inspire a renaissance in medical education. Dr. Drouin's work at Quantum University, with collaboration from pro-consciousness leaders such as Dr. Amit Goswami, Dr. Bruce Lipton, Dr. Joe Dispenza and many others, also charts a new foundation for medical instructions based on the updated model of the science of quantum physics.

From socio-economic reorganization, to technology-enabled evaluation and preventive care supporting a positive lifestyle, this path promises a future that dismantles current linear models of thinking. As healthcare practitioners, we need to re-center our thinking around the full potential of the individual. We need to use multi-pronged approaches to finding the true causes of patients' physical, emotional (vital), psychological (mental) and spiritual (supramental) wellbeing in order to address the root-causes of their imbalances.

Paralleling Drouin and Goswami's work, Dr. Bruce Lipton comes from an entirely different perspective to contribute to the empirical science that lays consciousness as the foundation of healing. He goes a step further to provide insight into the biology of how genetic data becomes read and expressed. Dr. Lipton's science takes us "from victim to creator." It shows us how central we are in creating our lives.

Trained in cell culturing, Dr. Lipton started cloning stem cells in 1968 under the guidance of Dr. Irv Konigsberg who created the first stem cell cultures. Experimentation led to a peculiar outcome -- the environment changed and determined the birth of new cells. Muscle progenitor cells sometimes stayed as muscle, sometimes become bone or fat cells. Genes, therefore, do not determine the formation of cells. Dr. Lipton also views each one of the 50+ trillion cells in our bodies as a living, sentient individuals with their own purpose, living within a community. Health is a function of the harmony within that community.

In today's world, where individualized genetic research is touted as the end-all in therapy -- from weightloss to alcoholism -- we must consider the history behind the Human Genome Project. Paul Silverman, one of the lead architects of the project, disclosed that the researchers were sponsored by venture capitalists, expecting to discover 150,000+ genes -- one for each of the 100,000 proteins in the body, plus about 50,000 genes controlling the other genes. Each sequence was to be patented and sold to pharmaceutical companies. 150,000 genes leading to 150,000 new medicines were expected to bring in a vast amount of wealth. The project had little to do human evolution and a lot to do with making money. The human genome stopped at uncovering only about 25,000 genes with no mention of the 100,000+ expected missing genes.

In addition, gene expression is controlled by receptors. Each gene is a program. Cell membranes function just like information processors. Unique, identifying protein keys called receptors live on the surface of our cells. These keys respond to environmental information -- what comes in and what stays out. Our receptors function as antennas that pick up broadcasts. That is how gene expression is determined. That is the essence of the science of epigenetics -- the controls above the controls. And we are the broadcasts. We control our cells. Specifically, not "we" but our perceptions.

Receptors can create perceptions, and perceptions change receptors, as receptor cells are changed by stimulus. A transmembrane protein receptor, for example, is a cell membrane protein that creates a physiological change in a neuron. This usually happens through cell signaling or through opening of ion channels. Transmembrane receptors are thus activated by perception.

The sensation of touch and perception are also closely related. Sensation is data collected by sensory receptors, and perception is how the brain selects, organizes, and interprets these sensations. Each individual brain interprets stimuli differently. That interpretation is based on history, learning, experience, memory, emotions, and expectations.

Quantum physics supports all of this as well, as it reveals only energy beneath our apparent physicality. We are not separate from our environment or from each other, posits quantum entanglement. The future of medicine brings the quantum world into focus. The reductionist thinking of the mechanical world is marred by limitations. Biological processes are quantum processes and should be treated as such. Our environment is an energy field and it is "everything from the core of being to the edge of the universe." -- Bruce Lipton, PhD

Spontaneous healing and the placebo effect are also quantum processes that boast scientific merit. The field of psychology claims as its own. Yet, there is scant regard or examination of the biological processes that must happen for mind-body medicine to be effective. Could you imagine the ramifications of controlling placebo outcomes via a structured scientific method? The placebo effect if the most wonderful part of healing -- it is side-effect free and it doesn't have to cost anything.

Why is placebo healing left to chance when it's a vital component of one's ability to recover? Why do most mainstream studies start with bias right from the beginning? Professor Ted Kaptchuk of Harvard-affiliated Beth Israel Deaconess Medical Center, for example, conducted a study that showed a migraine placebo medication being 50% effective due to the ritual of imbibing a pill periodically. This process, he believes, triggers an expectation or a belief in healing, which translates into a real, marked improvement.

> "...experts have concluded that reacting to a placebo is not proof that a certain treatment doesn't work, but rather that another, non-pharmacological mechanism may be present...How placebos work is still not quite understood, but it involves a complex neurobiological reaction that includes everything from increases in feel-good neurotransmitters, like endorphins and dopamine, to greater activity in certain brain regions linked to moods, emotional

reactions, and self-awareness. All of it can have therapeutic benefit." (Harvard 2017)

The power of the placebo effect, Published: May, 2017

Dr. Kaptchuk's research stops at placebo for pain, excluding physiological changes for chronic conditions, yet today, through quantum theory and specifically the New World View, we have an insight into the foundational science behind it. Dr. Amit Goswami has drawn a map of the road to conscious quantum jumping, and Dr. Bruce Lipton has revealed epigenetics, effectors, receptors and the physiological changes that occur prompted by belief. We know that spontaneous healing is real. The libraries are full of books, examples, and doctor accounts. Long accepted by ancient traditions as miracles of God (and in a sense they are), there are natural laws that can promulgate connecting to all-there-is, the nonlocality, source, spirit... [insert your choice of word for the Universal Force here]. A beautiful concept lay herein, one free of dogma, separation and even religion, one that makes us all part of the same.

The anti-inflammatory diet (food regimen)

The formula is basic, though it may have to be adjusted if allergies or sensitivities are present. Indulge in unsweetened, dairy-free, organic oatmeal for breakfast. For lunch and dinner, take a whole starch (brown rice, millet, buckwheat, quinoa, bulgur, potatoes and other root vegetables) and cover with raw or steamed array of veggies (the more colors, the better). Enjoy a legume soup and a green salad. Feel free to dress your meal with flavor: freshly squeezed lemon, balsamic glaze, a homemade miso/ginger sauce, garlic in walnut oil, mashed avocado with lime juice, caponata, pico de gallo, hummus or a veggie dip of some sort. Having these homemade, additive-free "dressings/sauces" on hand will save you a lot of prep time.

Minimize or work toward eliminating all dairy, red meat, oil of any kind, fried AND sautéed foods (throw out your frying pan), processed foods and refined sugars. Replace milk with almond milk, yogurt and/or non-dairy coconut yogurt. Substitute meat with beans whenever you would normally reach for chicken or steak. Hundred grams of black beans contain 21g of protein and 48% of iron.

Other rules of the road:

1. Start your morning with a glass of lemon water at room temperature. Do not eat for 30 minutes after.
2. Have fruit, a green smoothie, coconut yogurt or plain oatmeal for breakfast.
3. Eat vegetables of every color, legumes, fresh nuts or seeds.
4. Do not eat anything fried or sautéed. Raw, boiled, blanched, grilled or steamed foods only. No oil should be ever heated over or under your vegetables.
5. Eliminate all processed, prepared, canned and packaged foods. Avoid anything that comes in a box.
6. Eliminate or reduce meat, fish, eggs and dairy.

7. Eliminate refined sugars -- sweets, candy, drinks, soda, corn bread, white bread and white pasta.
8. Drink 3 - 4 cups of unsweetened green tea per day. Other easy-to-find hepatic cleansers include nettles, milk thistle and dandelion root. Consult with your physician for contraindications if you are taking medications of any type.
9. Take a daily multi-strain probiotic. Look for at least six varied bacteria strains.
10. A fully plant-based diet is recommended for 8 weeks. After that, 2-3 ounces of ricotta, yogurt, lean, organic, unprocessed meat cut, a sprinkle of feta or goat cheese can be added.

Sample Meal Plan

Monday

Breakfast: F*resh* berries of choice and organic oatmeal.
Lunch: Chopped boiled (or baked) red potatoes with fresh red onions and shredded carrots seasoned with mashed avocado blended with lemon juice and *iodized* sea salt and pepper.
Dinner: Amaranth, quinoa or millet with red beans topped with fresh tomatoes, cucumbers, avocados and parsley or cilantro. Green side salad (no dressing other than apple cider, balsamic vinegar or lemon juice).
Snack: Apple slices, walnuts, raw almonds. Top with sesame seeds.

Tuesday

Breakfast: Plain oatmeal with strawberries and bananas. Pure, dark chocolate chunks.
Lunch: Gnocchi topped with pesto, pine nuts, roasted red peppers, and asparagus.

Dinner: A bed of greens and boiled chopped red potatoes, topped with white beans, onions, broccoli (or red peppers) and fresh dill. Mustard and lemon juice dressing.

Snack: Celery sticks and hummus.

Wednesday

Breakfast: Ezekiel bread avocado toast. A glass of freshly squeezed juice.

Lunch: Brown rice, covered with curried chickpeas, sautéed mushrooms and fresh rosemary. Vegetarian chili.

Dinner: Bruschetta topped with fresh diced tomatoes, onions, parsley and balsamic vinegar dressing. Pasta fagioli soup.

Snack: Vegetarian taco.

Thursday

Breakfast: Smoothie with almond milk, apples, celery, parsley, and bananas.

Lunch: Quinoa with sundried tomatoes, fresh onions, mushrooms and fresh basil. Season and top with nutritional yeast and lemon juice to taste. Minestrone soup.

Dinner: Eggplant marinara on a whole wheat sub, Ezekiel bread or wrap or over a bed of greens. Lentil soup.

Snack: Carrot or red pepper sticks and bean dip. A cup of kombucha.

Friday

Breakfast: Fruit salad, plain oatmeal or a green drink. Avocado toast.

Lunch: Zucchini or bean noodles topped with vodka sauce, mushrooms, garlic, onions, and fresh basil.

Dinner: Miso soup. Brown rice, avocado and cucumber sushi; seaweed salad.

Snack: Black bean soup.

Saturday

Breakfast: Buckwheat crepes with fresh fruit and pure maple syrup or raw honey.

Lunch: Lentil or pea soup with whole wheat pita bread. Lettuce, onion, tomato, cucumber and avocado salad.

Dinner: Vegetable soup (or kimchee). Falafel.

Snack: Fresh broccoli bites (or fresh zucchini) dipped in hummus.

Sunday

Breakfast: Plain granola with walnuts and agave.

Lunch: Spanish rice (brown) and beans topped with tomatoes, onions and cilantro. Ginger-lime dressing. (Take a handful of pickled ginger and throw it in the blender with a swig of lime juice. Add salt and flaxseed oil to taste.)

Dinner: Veggie wrap with Portobello mushrooms, roasted red peppers, bean sprouts, onions and pesto. Dip: Balsamic vinegar blended with a spoonful of raw honey and wholegrain mustard. Lentil soup.

Snack: Roasted yams or sautéed green beans with salt, lemon and garlic.

Managing expectations

Since health improvement relies on bioenergetic dynamism, its workings are much like those of acupuncture -- slow and continual. Diet is key. Pay attention to your body and visit an integrative health practitioner. People with long-settled chronic conditions or those who re-injure muscles or ligaments due to occupational hazard may need to follow a treatment plan for life. Many may not experience relief until 12 months following a treatment plan. Patients with non-medication induced fibromyalgia and certain types of arthritis, on the other hand, often experience full or near full recovery if they are diligent with their diet over time.

Patients who are battling certain conditions, choose to remain plant based. Others, remain plant based on moral grounds. Whatever your motivation, follow your heart, love your anatomy as is, and listen to your body. Only a few days of non-compliance bring about the return of joint pain and inflammation for many. I am one of them. I choose a pain-free life.

Side note: Please familiarize yourselves with the ins and outs of plant-based eating, proper B12 supplementation. Make sure your nutrient intake is adequate. Consult your physician (MD).

The 3-day juice detox

Detox, short for detoxification, is the body's way of neutralizing and eliminating toxins. Since the liver, intestines, kidneys, lungs, skin, blood, and lymphatic systems work together in this regard, many of the individual organ detoxes may be bundled.

I usually do this detox when my system feels sluggish. If no contraindications are present, it's a good way to jumpstart any new regimen. I decided to share my individual experience here in order to avoid spiraling down a vortex of thoughts, ideas, regimens and methods that address a multitude of problems and conditions.

The detox styles are many. Before I venture into mine, please note that if you decide to go down this path, you should be consulting your physician.

I do a juice fast that lasts three days. Some people do a week, two weeks, some even longer. I know an evolved yoga practitioner (and a kind soul) who does not eat every Monday for many, many decades now. He says that he is just letting his system rest.

My three-day fasts started when I was a teenager and they were recommended by my gymnastics coach, who told us that we will feel better, have clear skin and more energy if we just drank lemon water for three days each month starting during full moon. And we trained like crazy during these times too. These were pre-coffee days. Today I drink my coffee to avoid withdrawal headaches. I also drink various freshly squeezed juices, blends and smoothies.

I also add 30 minutes of infrared sauna sessions at the end of each fasting day. If you don't have a sauna, do warm epsom salt foot soaks, while sipping hot nettle tea. Wrap your body in two-three heavy blankets to induce sweating. Do not do this before consulting your physician.

Since I am already plant-based, I do not add a nutritional element after the three days are over. I recommend that my patients do (with doctor's approval).

The Role of PT

All of this talk about nutrition...what about exercise? Whether you are exerting physical or emotional stress over your body, your glands will be the first responders. They will release the chemicals and hormones responsible for controlling your emotional or physiological changes.

Ever wonder why after a certain age people are prone to gaining weight without changing their caloric intake? Although this issue is much more complex than placing blame on the endocrine system, among other factors, the body starts preparing for the impending bone density loss, which is bound to happen with age. Fat is being stored to protect your body with cushioning adipose tissue. This is a precautionary function, and even if your bone loss tests are normal, the body charges on.

Exercise is beneficial not only for your heart and internal organs, but it also has a measured effect on how old you look and feel.

- During exercise, your pituitary gland releases human growth hormone (HGH), which increases bone, muscle and tissue repair.
- Exercise stimulates the thyroid gland, which sends out hormones that regulate metabolism, body temperature, heart rate, kidney functioning, blood pressure, etc. Did you know that that the thyroid also controls focus and concentration?
- Your adrenal glands are also significantly affected by exercise. Since they are responsible for the release of cortisol into the bloodstream (cortisol controls blood pressure, glucose, inflammation, hydration and your ability to cope with pressure) these glands play a major role in your wellbeing.
- Exercise improves insulin sensitivity, which gives the body a feeling of being satiated when properly nourished. Since insulin regulates glucose (blood

sugar) by transporting it to muscles and tissues, increased sensitivity means lowered risk for obesity and diabetes.

- Exercise also induces testosterone, which can increase one's confidence, drive and libido.

I recommend that you consult with a Physical Therapist prior to engaging in any new exercise regimen.

Although I believe that there are highly qualified personal trainers, enlisting the help of a medical professional will take your routine to a whole new level.

Treating the body as a whole

We live in amazing times. Due to the speed of information, we have center stage seating at the arena of the socio-economic structure of reorganization. On one hand, we have a shift from traditional industry to a digital revolution, on the other, we have more, better and faster new technologies. In addition, the information age has created a knowledge-based society allowing people to explore anything and everything that can be used to improve their lives -- from jobs, nutrition and exercise to medications and alternative treatments. That is not to say that any of this is new. On the contrary, there have been many paths to healing since the dawn of civilization. The only difference today stems from the ease with which we can find information. And that is only half the story. All and any information we find can be traced back to scientific research, experiential proof and case studies.

This is vital to our survival. It means empowerment and self-responsibility. It means exploring different venues and keeping an open mind. It means access to the thinking of some of the greatest minds in the world today -- healers, quantum physicists, psychologists and naturopaths interested in looking at the individual holistically, as a functional unit comprising thoughts, emotions, cognitive behavior, lifestyle needs, spiritual convictions, loves and fears.

The reductionist mentality of addressing symptoms rather than causes -- albeit its fantastic short term solutions -- is going away. Those who seek shall find. The world belongs to a kinder, gentler future not only in a way of how we treat those around us, but how we treat the 50+ trillion cells in our own bodies. The outer world is a reflection of what is transpiring in our inner worlds, and we now have access to a greater number of potentialities to choose from. When Francis Bacon said, "knowledge is power," did he realize he was describing quantum probability enhancement created by the power of a new envisioned future of reality that doesn't currently exist? Intuitively he described new photon forms injected into our present via new knowledge networks and creative imagination. We no longer have to choose from realms of limited scope. Our vision can engage and create a new outcome for our condition, supercharged by new data, and by staying patient, humble and keeping the greater good in mind.

The future of quantum medicine -- a). nutrition as a science of quantum processes, b). light and sound technologies -- is bright. From brain mapping to magnetic microbots, we are entering a crucial point in existence that may change everything -- our healthcare systems, social structures, politics and economics alike. Parasympathetic response, as a function of cellular self-repair and pain management, plays an important role in the next stage of treating causes rather than symptoms, and it should be added as a complement to most allopathic treatments. Its application -- via laser acupuncture, aromatherapy, far-infrared light therapy, vagus nerve stimulation, and other beautiful experiences designed to bathe all senses in bliss -- is a highly effective method that evokes supreme relaxation, so that the body can stay balanced and on track. The nutrition element further facilitates anti-inflammatory responses for providing long-term relief.

The universe is a vast space where everything is possible. Finding respite from the daily strives of our existence, while being gently guided to infuse our experiences with prana, is a treat for the mind, body and spirit alike. Here is to empowering our senses and claiming the divinity within.

References

American Pain Society (2012), Chronic pain costs U.S. up to $635 billion, study shows. *Science Daily*. Retrieved July 3, 2018 from https://www.sciencedaily.com/releases/2012/09/120911091100.htm

Arthritis Foundation. More fiber, less inflammation? Eating a high-fiber diet may help reduce inflammation. Retrieved July 15, 2018 from https://www.arthritis.org/living-with-arthritis/arthritis-diet/anti-inflammatory/fiber-inflammation.php

Asher, Gary N. MD, MPH, Jonas, Daniel E, MD, MPH, Coeytaux, Remy R, MD, PhD, Reilly, Aimee C, LAc, Loh, Yen L. MD, Motsinger-Reif, Alison A., PhD and Windham, Stacey J., MS (2016). Auriculotherapy for pain management: a systematic review and meta-analysis of randomized controlled trials. *PMC, US National Library of Medicine.*

Retrieved July 5, 2018 from https://www.ncbi.nlm.nih.gov/pmc/articles/PMC3110838/

Avci, Pinar, MD, Gupta, Asheesh, PhD, Sadasivam, Magesh MTech, Vecchio, Daniela, PhD, Pam, Zeev, MD, Pam, Nadav, MD, and Hamblin, Michael R, PhD (2013). Low-level laser (light) therapy (LLLT) in skin: stimulating, healing, restoring. *Scmsjournal.com.* Reprinted by PCM, US National Library of Medicine. Retrieved July 7, 2018 from https://www.ncbi.nlm.nih.gov/pmc/articles/PMC4126803/

Barbault, Pasche (2013, November). Targeted treatment of cancer with radiofrequency electromagnetic fields amplitude-modulated at tumor-specific frequencies. *PMC, US National Library of Medicine.* Retrieved July 11, 2018 from https://www.ncbi.nlm.nih.gov/pmc/articles/PMC3845545/

Bargh, Morsella (2008, January 1). The unconscious mind. *Perspectives on Psychological Science.* Retrieved August 20, 2018 from http://journals.sagepub.com/doi/abs/10.1111/j.1745-6916.2008.00064.x?url_ver=Z39.88-2003&rfr_id=ori:rid:crossref.org&rfr_dat=cr_pub%3dpubmed

Beaty, Delicia and Foutch, Sharon (2009, October 13) The benefits of soaking nuts and seeds. *Food Matters.* Retrieved August 22, 2018 from https://www.foodmatters.com/article/the-benefits-of-soaking-nuts-and-seeds

Borovikova LV1, Ivanova S, Zhang M, Yang H, Botchkina GI, Watkins LR, Wang H, Abumrad N, Eaton JW, Tracey KJ. (2000, May 25) Vagus nerve stimulation attenuates the systemic inflammatory response to endotoxin. *Nature.* Retrieved July 7, 2018 from https://www.ncbi.nlm.nih.gov/pubmed/10839541/

Campbell, T. Colin Center for Nutrition Studies (2017). The China study. Retrieved July 13,

2018 from https://nutritionstudies.org/the-china-study/

Cassata, Cathy (2016, February 19). What is vasopressin? *Everyday Health.* Retrieved July 2, 2018 from https://www.everydayhealth.com/vasopressin/guide/

Chevalier, Gaetan (2018) Connecting with science. *Earthing Institute.* Retrieved August 22, 2018 from http://www.earthinginstitute.net/research/

Cinelli, Mark A (2014, January 24). Cortisol: a powerful stress hormone and how it could affect your body. *Boston Herald.* Retrieved July 2, 2018 from http://www.bostonherald.com/entertainment/health_fitness/mr_fit/2014/01/cortisol_a_powerful_stress_hormone_how_it_can_

Coles, Lauren (2016, October 25). 3 reasons why office yoga works. *Huffington Post.* Retrieved July 1, 2018 from https://www.huffingtonpost.com/lauren-coles/3-reasons-why-office-yoga_b_12624964.html

Conrad-Stoppler, Melissa MD. Endorphins: natural pain and stress and fighters. *Medicine Net.* Retrived July 3, 2018 from https://www.medicinenet.com/endorphins_natural_pain_and_stress_fighters/views.htm

Difference BTW author (2016, June 19). Difference between sympathetic and parasympathetic system. *Difference BTW.* Retrieved August 22, 2018 from https://www.differencebtw.com/difference-between-sympathetic-and-parasympathetic-nerve-system/

Dispenza, Joe (2014) United in blooms of consciousness, *Dr. Joe Dispenza's Blog.* Retrieved August 22, 2018 from https://www.drjoedispenza.com/blog/category/quantum-field/

Dolphin Neurostim. How does acupuncture work even without needles? *Dolphinmps.com*.
    Retrieved July 5, 2018 from https://www.dolphinmps.com/acupuncture-benefits/

Donaldson, Michael S, Speight, Neal, Loomis Stephen (2001, September 26). Fibromyalgia
    syndrome improved using a mostly raw vegetarian diet: an observational study. *PMC, US*
    National Library of Medicine. Retrieved on July 19, 2018

https://www.ncbi.nlm.nih.gov/pmc/articles/PMC57816/
Drouin, Dr. Paul. The science of spontaneous healing. *DrPaulDrouin.com*. Retrieved on July 21,
    2018 from https://drpauldrouin.com/science-of-spontaneous-healing/
Drouin, Dr. Paul. A positive and inspiring vision for healthcare. *DrPaulDrouin.com*. Retrieved
    on July 21, 2018 from

https://drpauldrouin.com/a-positive-and-inspiring-vision-for-health-care/

Drouin, Dr. Paul. The challenge for pro-consciousness medicine. *DrPaulDrouin.com*. Retrieved
    on August 22, 2018 from
    https://drpauldrouin.com/the-challenge-for-pro-consciousness-medicine/

Edgar Cayce Cures. The violet ray. *EdgarCayceCures.com*. Retrieved July 11, 2018 from
    https://edgarcaycecures.com/violet-ray/

Edwards, Michael. (2015, May 17) What causes chronic inflammation, and how to stop it for
    good. *Organic Lifestyle Magazine.* Retrieved July 12, 2018 from
    http://www.organiclifestylemagazine.com/issue/15-what-causes-chronic-inflammation-and-how-to-stop-it-for-good

Falk, Dan (2016). New support for alternative quantum view. *Quanta Magazine.* Retrieved July
    5, 2018 from

https://www.quantamagazine.org/pilot-wave-theory-gains-experimental-support-20160516/

Felman, Adam (2017, July 27) What is pain and how do we treat it? *Medical News Today*. Retrieved August 22, 2018 from https://www.medicalnewstoday.com/articles/145750.php

Fornasari, Diego (2014) Pain pharmacology: focus on opiods. *PMC, US National Library of Medicine*. Retrieved August 22, 2018 from https://www.ncbi.nlm.nih.gov/pmc/articles/PMC4269136/

Garfield, Leanna (2016, October 18) 18 European countries where people work fewer hours than the US. *Business Insider*. Retrieved June 21, 2018 from http://www.businessinsider.com/countries-that-work-least-and-most-hours-2016-10

Gatchel, Rober PhD, Howard, Krista PhD (2018, April) The Biopsychosocial Approach.

Practical Pain Management. Retrieved September 6, 2018 from

https://www.practicalpainmanagement.com/treatments/psychological/biopsychosocial-approach

Goswami, Amit (2013, August 13). Health, healing, and quantum physics. *AmitGoswami.org.* Retrieved July 20, 2018

http://www.amitgoswami.org/2013/08/13/health-healing-quantum-physics/

Greger, Michael MD (2012, September 20) How does meat cause inflammation? *Nutrition Facts.* Retrieved July 18, 2018 from

https://nutritionfacts.org/2012/09/20/why-meat-causes-inflammation/

Greger, Michael MD. Rheumatoid Arthritis. *Nutrition Facts.* Retrieved July 18, 2018 from

https://nutritionfacts.org/topics/rheumatoid-arthritis/

Hart, Tobin (2014) The Integrative Mind, p.43. Retrieved August 22, 2018 from https://books.google.com/books?id=mVgtBAAAQBAJ&pg=PA43&lpg=PA43&dq=bohm+all+patterns+repeat+and+interconnected&source=bl&ots=di9v2FLgLv&sig=Nn0zrR0XXmIKFDmRZFAV54Hbi2M&hl=en&sa=X&ved=2ahUKEwj-iPHQqPLcAhUpwFkKHVxcCFUQ6AEwAXoECAkQAQ#v=onepage&q=bohm%20all%20patterns%20repeat%20and%20interconnected&f=false

Harvard Medical School Staff (2018, May 1). Understanding the stress response. *Harvard Health Publishing*. Retrieved July 2, 2018 from https://www.health.harvard.edu/staying-healthy/understanding-the-stress-response

Harvard Medical School Staff (2017, May). The power of the placebo effect. *Harvard Health Publishing*. Retrieved July 3, 2018 from https://www.health.harvard.edu/mental-health/the-power-of-the-placebo-effect

Health Direct authors. Pain Relief Medicines. *Health Direct*. Retrieved August 22, 2018 from
https://www.healthdirect.gov.au/pain-relief-medicines

Hoffman, Matthew MD (2014). Picture of Blood. *WebMD.com*. Retrieved August 22, 2018 from
https://www.webmd.com/heart/anatomy-picture-of-blood#1

Horgan, Joe (2014, July 14). Scientific heretic Rupert Sheldrake on morphic fields, psychic dogs and other mysteries. *Scientific American Blog*. Retrieved August 22, 2018 from
https://blogs.scientificamerican.com/cross-check/scientific-heretic-rupert-sheldrake-on-morphic-fields-psychic-dogs-and-other-mysteries/

Houchins, Joe. Are prescription painkillers as addictive as heroin? *Drugabuse.com*. Retrieved July 3, 2018 from
https://drugabuse.com/library/painkiller-addiction/

Johns Hopkins Medicine. The brain-gut connection. *John Hopkins University Press*. Retrieved

July 14, 2018 from https://www.hopkinsmedicine.org/health/healthy_aging/healthy_body/the-brain-gut-connection

Johnson, Reilly (2017, July 24) How to naturally increase dopamine, serotonin and endorphins depleted by opioid addiction. *Opiate Freedom Center.* Retrieved July 18, 2018 from https://opiate-freedom-center.com/opioid-addiction-naturally-increase-your-bodies-endorphins-serotonin/

Kaku, Michio (2017) The bizarre and wonderful world of quantum theory—and how understanding it has ultimately changed our lives. Big Think. Retrieved August 22, 2018 from https://bigthink.com/dr-kakus-universe/the-bizarre-and-wonderful-world-of-quantum-theory-and-how-understanding-it-has-ultimately-changed-our-lives

Kegel, Magdalena (2016, November 28). Chronic inflammation may explain heart disease in rheumatoid arthritis. *Rheumatoid Arthritis News.* Retrieved July 13, 2018 from
https://rheumatoidarthritisnews.com/2016/11/28/chronic-heart-inflammation-explain-heart-disease-rheumatoid-arthritis/

Kecskes, Alex A. How massage can benefit your heart. *Pacific College Press.* Retrieved July 19, 2018 from
https://www.pacificcollege.edu/news/blog/2014/11/04/how-massage-can-benefit-your-heart

Klabunde, Richard E (2016, December 8). Vasopressin (antidiuretic hormone). *Cardiovascular Physiology Concepts.* Retrieved July 2, 2018 from
https://www.cvphysiology.com/Blood%20Pressure/BP016

Knox, Sarah M., Lombaert, Isabelle M. A., Haddox, Candace L., Abrams, Shaun R., Cotrim,

Ana, Wilson, Adrian J., Hoffman, Matthew P. (2013, February 19). Parasympathetic stimulation improves epithelial organ regeneration. *Nature Communications.* Volume 4. Retrieved July 1, 2018 from https://www.ncbi.nlm.nih.gov/pmc/articles/PMC3582394/

Korb, Alex PhD (2012, November 20) The grateful brain. The neuroscience of giving thanks. *Psychology Today.* Retrieved July 20, 2018 https://www.psychologytoday.com/us/blog/prefrontal-nudity/201211/the-grateful-brain

Kuboyama, N, Ohta, M, Sato, Y, Abiko, Y (2014) Anti-inflammatory activities of light emitting diode irradiation on collagen-induced arthritis in mice (a secondary publication). *Laser Therapy Journal.* Volume 23. Reprinted by PMC, US National Library of Medicine. Retrieved July 7, 2018 from https://www.ncbi.nlm.nih.gov/pmc/articles/PMC4215126/

Langford, Kimberly (2008, June 12). High frequency facial treatment for acne & aging skin.
Jellen Products. Retrieved July 11, 2018 from
https://www.jellenproducts.com/high-frequency-facial-treatment/

Lesch, Susan (2018, March 28). The Relaxation Response. *Wikipedia.* Retrieved July 1, 2018
from
https://en.wikipedia.org/wiki/The_Relaxation_Response
Lipton, Bruce PhD (2012, June 7). The wisdom of your cells. *BruceLipton.com.* Retrieved July
21, 2018 from
https://www.brucelipton.com/resource/article/the-wisdom-your-cells Lumen Learning. Sensory perception: taste and olfaction. Retrieved July 21, 2018 from
https://courses.lumenlearning.com/ap1/chapter/sensory-perception/
Lumen Learning. Module 5: sensation and perception. Retrieved July 23, 2018 from

https://courses.lumenlearning.com/wmopen-psychology/chapter/outcome-sensation-and-perception/

Mayo Clinic Staff (2016, April 21). Chronic stress puts your health at risk. *Mayo Clinic*. Retrieved July 1, 2018 from https://www.mayoclinic.org/healthy-lifestyle/stress-management/in-depth/stress/art-20046037

McDougall, John. Walter Kempner, MD -- founder of the rice diet. *Dr. McDougall's Health and Medical Center*. Retrieved July 3, 2018 from https://www.drmcdougall.com/2013/12/31/walter-kempner-md-founder-of-the-rice-diet/)

Manning, Khakimov, Dall & Truscott (2015, May 25) Wheeler's delayed-choice gedanken experiment with a single atom. *Nature*. Volume 11, pages 539-542 Retrieved July 19, 2018 from https://www.nature.com/articles/nphys3343

Mental Health America authors (2018). Work life balance. *Mental Health America.* Retrieved August 22, 2018 from http://www.mentalhealthamerica.net/work-life-balance

Mercante, Beniamina, Deriu, Franca and Ragnon, Claire-Marie (2018) Auricular neuromodulation: the emerging concept beyond the stimulation of vagus and trigeminal nerves. *PMC, US National Library of Medicine.* Retrieved July 5, 2018 from https://www.ncbi.nlm.nih.gov/pmc/articles/PMC5874575/

Mercola, Dr. Joseph (2010, November 23). Top 10 food additives to avoid. *Food Matters.* Retrieved July 11, 2018 from https://www.foodmatters.com/article/top-10-food-additives-to-avoid

Miller, G. E (January 2, 2018) The US is the most overworked developed nation in the world. *20*

Something Finance. Retrieved August 22, 2018 from https://20somethingfinance.com/american-hours-worked-productivity-vacation/

Milne, Robert MD and Sorgnard, Richard PhD. Quantum theory underpins electromagnetic

therapies for pain management. *Practical Pain Management*, Volume 13, Issue 1. Retrieved August 22, 2018 from https://www.practicalpainmanagement.com/treatments/complementary/magnets/quantum-theory-underpins-electromagnetic-therapies-pain-management

National Cancer Institute (2016). Parasympathetic nervous system, *PubMed Health.* Retrieved August 22, 2018 from https://www.ncbi.nlm.nih.gov/pubmedhealth/PMHT0025459/

Nielsen, Arya PhD (2015, May 5). The science of gua sha. *Pacific College Press*. Retrieved July 9, 2018 from https://www.pacificcollege.edu/news/press-releases/2015/05/05/science-gua-sha

NRDC. Toxic chemicals. Retrieved July 14, 2018 from https://www.nrdc.org/issues/toxic-chemicals

O'Rahilli, Muller, Carpenter, Swenson (2004) Basic Human Anatomy, Chapter 3, *Dartmouth Medical School*. Retrieved August 22, 2018 from https://www.dartmouth.edu/~humananatomy/part_1/chapter_3.html

Organic Facts authors (2013). 20 Amazing Benefits & Uses Of Cabbage. *OrganicFacts.net*. Retrieved July 18, 2018 from https://www.organicfacts.net/health-benefits/vegetable/health-benefits-of-cabbage.html

Oxford Economics (2017) Infographic - the problem with burnout. Society for Human Resource Management. Retrieved august 22, 2018 from https://www.shrm.org/hr-today/news/hr-magazine/0817/pages/infographic-the-problem-with-burnout.aspx

Ranabir, Salam, Reetu, K. (2011) Stress and hormones. *PMC: US National Library of Medicine.* Retrieved July 3, 2018 from https://www.ncbi.nlm.nih.gov/pmc/articles/PMC3079864/

Rensselaer Polytechnic Institute. Full spectrum light sources, case study. *Rensselaer.* Retrieved July 11, 2018 from http://www.lrc.rpi.edu/programs/nlpip/lightinganswers/fullspectrum/casestudy.asp

Rice University. Antioxidants and free radicals. *Rice University Press.* Retrieved July 15, 2018 from https://www.rice.edu/~jenky/sports/antiox.html

Schawbel, Dan (2017, October 23) Richard Branson: his views on entrepreneurship, well-being and work friendships. *Forbes Magazine.* Retrieved August 22, 2018 from https://www.forbes.com/sites/danschawbel/2017/10/23/richard-branson-his-views-on-entrepreneurship-well-being-and-work-friendships/#1e0d07eb55d2

ScienCentral, Inc, and The American Institute of Physics (1999). Quantum Mechanics. *PBS.* Retrived on July 19th from http://www.pbs.org/transistor/science/info/quantum.html

Seymore, Tom (2017, June 28). Everything you need to know about the vagus nerve. *Medical News Today.* Retrieved July 7, 2018 from

https://www.medicalnewstoday.com/articles/318128.php

Shape Editors. 7 surprising ways junk food makes you miserable. *Shape Magazine.* Retrieved August 22, 2018 from https://www.shape.com/healthy-eating/diet-tips/7-surprising-ways-junk-food-makes-you-miserable

Shen-nong Authors (2005). What are the seven emotions? *Shen-Nong.* Retrieved August 22,

2018 from http://www.shen-nong.com/eng/principles/sevenemotions.html

Shnitkind E, Yaping E, Geen S, Shalita AR, Lee WL. (2006) Anti-inflammatory properties of narrow-band blue light. *Laser Therapy Journal.* Reprinted by PMC, US National Library of Medicine. Retrieved July 7, 2018 from https://www.ncbi.nlm.nih.gov/pubmed/16865864

Smarter Healing authors (2018) Acupuncture Points. *Smarter Healing.* Retrieved August 22, 2018 from https://www.smarterhealing.com/acupuncture-points/

Smith, Lori (2017) What are binaural beats and how do they work? *Medical News Today.* Retrieved July 3, 2018 from https://www.medicalnewstoday.com/articles/320019.php

Soveyd N, Abdolahi M, Bitarafan S, Tafakhori A, Sarraf P, Togha M, Okhovat AA, Hatami M,

Sedighiyan M, Djalali M, Mohammadzadeh Honarvar N (2017). Molecular mechanisms of omega-3 fatty acids in migraine headaches. *PMC, US National Library of Medicine.* Retrieved July 18, 2018 from https://www.ncbi.nlm.nih.gov/pmc/articles/PMC5937007/

Spritzler, Franziska RD, CDE (2017, June 3). 6 foods that cause inflammation. *Healthline.* Retrieved July 18, 2018 from https://www.healthline.com/nutrition/6-foods-that-cause-inflammation#section1

Starwinn, Darren OMD LAC (2004, April) "As above, so below," Acupuncture: great loops and reverse body image points. *Acupuncture Today*, Volume 5, Issue 4. Retrieved August 22, 2018 from https://www.acupuncturetoday.com/mpacms/at/article.php?id=28439

The Truth authors. Every 12 minutes someone in America dies from an opioid overdose. *The*

Truth. Retrieved August 22, 2018 from https://opioids.thetruth.com/o/about

Tricoles, Robin (2017, March 1). Treatment of pain gets the green light. *UA News, Journal of the University of Arizona.* Retrieved July 7, 2018 from https://uanews.arizona.edu/story/treatment-pain-gets-green-light

University of Toronto. (2005, December 7). Inflammation linked to chronic pain: study. *ScienceDaily.* Retrieved July 13, 2018 from www.sciencedaily.com/releases/2005/12/051207083822.htm

Vitality Link Finder (2011, December 6). New Developments in color therapy: acupuncture meridians facilitate the body's absorption of light. Part 1. *Vitality Link.* Retrieved July 7, 2018 from http://www.vitalitylink.com/article-addiction-and-abuse-treatment-and-healing-702-devel

opments-color-therapy-acupuncture-meridians-facilitate

Voigt, John. The Emotions. *ChineseMedicineLiving.com*. Retrieved July 5, 2018 from
https://www.chinesemedicineliving.com/philosophy/the-emotions/

Watkins, Thayer. The advanced technology of ancient China. *San Jose State University Department of Economics*. Retrieved July 7, 2018 from
http://www.sjsu.edu/faculty/watkins/ancientchina.htm

Watson, Stephanie (2017) Fibromyalgia diet: foods to ease symptoms. *Healthline.* Retrieved August 22, 2018 from
https://www.healthline.com/health/fibromyalgia-diet-to-ease-symptoms#foods-to-avoid

WebMD authors. What is inflammation? *WebMD.com* Retrieved August 22, 2018 from https://www.webmd.com/arthritis/about-inflammation#1

WebMD authors. What causes fibromyalgia? *WebMD.com.* Retrieved July 20, 2018 from

https://www.webmd.com/fibromyalgia/guide/fibromyalgia-causes

Wikipedia (2018, August 5) Big Bounce. Retrieved August 22, 2018 from

https://en.wikipedia.org/wiki/Big_Bounce

Wikipedia via Science Daily. Sympathetic nervous system. *Science Daily.* Retrieved August 22, 2018 from

https://www.sciencedaily.com/terms/sympathetic_nervous_system.htm

Wikipedia (2013, October 7) Violet Ray. Retrieved on July 11, 2018 from

https://en.wikipedia.org/wiki/Violet_ray

Wolchover, Natalie (2011, March 25). Afraid of needles? Poke-free acupuncture works just as well. *Live Science.* Retrieved July 7, 2018 from https://www.livescience.com/13419-afraid-needles-poke-free-acupuncture-works.html

Wolters Kluwer Health: Lippincott, Williams and Wilkins. (2016, October 28). High-frequency spinal cord stimulation provides better results in chronic back, leg pain. *ScienceDaily*. Retrieved July 18, 2018 from www.sciencedaily.com/releases/2016/10/161028125354.htm

Wong RA, Schumann B, Townsend R, Phelps CA. (2007) A survey of therapeutic ultrasound use by physical therapists who are orthopaedic certified specialists. PubMed.gov. Retrieved July 9, 2018 from https://www.ncbi.nlm.nih.gov/pubmed/17553923/

Wyatt, Myers. Are food additives aggravating your fibromyalgia? *Everyday Health PC Magazine*. Retrieved July 19, 2018 from https://www.everydayhealth.com/fibromyalgia/are-food-additives-aggravating-your-fibro

myalgia.aspx

Zimmerman, Jimenez, Pennison, Brezovich, Morgan, Mudry, Costa, Barbault, Pasche (2013, November). Targeted treatment of cancer with radiofrequency electromagnetic fields amplitude-modulated at tumor-specific frequencies. *PMC, US National Library of Medicine.* Retrieved July 11, 2018 from https://www.ncbi.nlm.nih.gov/pmc/articles/PMC3845545/

Made in the USA
Middletown, DE
19 January 2020